Surfing for Success
in Economics 1997

a student's guide to the INTERNET

Surfing for Success in Economics 1997

a student's guide to the INTERNET

Scott Simkins

**North Carolina Agricultural and
Technical State University**

Jim Barbour

Elon College

Andrew T. Stull

Prentice Hall
Upper Saddle River, NJ 07458

Development: Joan Waxman and Steve Deitmer
Interior design and formatting: Lorraine Patsco, Omegatype
Cover design: Lorraine Castellano
Advertising copy and design: Sheila Lynch and Eve Adams
Production manager: Richard Bretan
Manufacturing manager: Vincent Scelta

© 1998 by Prentice Hall, Inc.
A Simon & Schuster Company
Upper Saddle River, New Jersey 07458

Printed in the United States of America

10 9 8 7 6 5 4 3 2 1

ISBN: 0-13-648452-2

TRADEMARK INFORMATION
Air America is a trademark of SPRY Incorporated
America Online is a registered trademark of Quantum Computer Services Incorporated
Cello is a trademark of Cornell Law School
CompuServe is a trademark of CompuServe, Incorporated
Delphi is a trademark of Delphi Internet Services Incorporated
Enhanced NCSA Mosaic is a trademark of Spyglass Incorporated
eWorld is a trademark of Apple Computer Incorporated
InterAp is a trademark of California Software Incorporated
Java is a registered trademark of Sun Microsystems
Lycos is a trademark of Carnegie Mellon University
Microsoft Windows and *Microsoft Internet Explorer* are trademarks of Microsoft Corporation
NCSA Mosaic is a trademark of the National Center for Supercomputing Applications
NetCruiser is a trademark of Netcom On-Line CommunicationsServices Incorporated
Netscape Navegator is a registered trademark of Netscape Communications Corporation
Prodigy is a registered trademark of Prodigy Systems Incorpoated
Web Crawler is a trademark of Excite Incorporated
Web Explorer is a trademark of IBM Corporation
WinTapestry is a trademark of Frontier Technologies Corporation
WinWeb is a trademark of EINet Corporation
Yahoo! is a tardemark of Yahoo! Incorporated

The author and publisher of this manual have used their best efforts in preparing this book. The author and publisher make no warranty of any kind, expressed or implied, with regard to these programs or the documentation contained in this book. The author and publisher shall not be liable in any event for incidental or consequential damages in connection with, or arising out of, the furnishing, performance, or use of the programs described in this book.

Contents

Introduction

So you're taking a course in Economics and your instructor has suggested that you use the Internet to complete your assignments or simply keep abreast of economic news. Now what? Some of you may have already made use of the information available on the Internet, but for those of you who haven't, take heart. The Internet is not as frightening as it appears.

The aim of this *Guide* is to introduce you to this wonderfully rich source of information and help you make the most of it. The *Guide* is meant to be interactive, and along the way we'll stop periodically so you can practice what you've learned. Above all we hope that you have fun exploring the information available on the Internet and use it to broaden your understanding of economics. The Internet provides a wonderful tool for obtaining a wide range of information, but remember that this information is useful only when you transform it into knowledge. We hope to show you not only how to find information that will be helpful in your course, but also how to use that information to enhance your knowledge of economics. The Internet can be a wonderful learning tool—make the most of it!

How Can the Internet Help Me in Economics?

Before you begin your exploration of the Internet, it's useful to understand how this new tool fits in with all the other tools economists use to make decisions and answer questions. You've probably already been introduced to a formal definition of economics: the study of the allocation of scarce resources among alternative and competing ends. Informally, economics is simply about "how we get things done when we can't do everything" or "how we make decisions about what to do when we can't do it all."

To make a choice about anything you need information about the alternatives available to you, a way to compile and organize that information, and a set of decision "rules" to help you sift through the information and reach a conclusion. An example might be helpful. Let's say you're trying to choose between two possible dates for the coming weekend. One prospective date has asked you to go to a movie; the other has asked you to go dancing. To make a decision about which date to accept, or to accept neither, you first gather information (Do I enjoy being with this person? Who is likely to be more fun or more interesting?), then you organize and compile this information (How many movies have I been to recently? Do I trust the person who told me that one of the prospective dates is a snob?). Finally, you apply your set of decision rules (Is this more likely to be the start of a long-term relationship or a one-time date? What am I looking for this weekend, a playful good time or a quiet evening?). Once you have gone through this process, one choice will likely emerge as the one that more closely fits what you are looking for, and you make your decision about which date, if any, to accept.

Whether you are choosing between two alternative dates for the coming weekend or whether you are deciding where to locate a factory, whether to go to graduate school, or which artist's work to put in your art gallery, the fundamental decision-making process is the same. In many cases, such as choosing a date, we do not *consciously* follow the formal decision-making process laid out above, but in the case of a business decision or a decision about attending graduate school, the process is often explicit.

Studying economics can provide you with a set of decision rules that will be helpful in making decisions both in your personal and in your professional life. Most students who take economics also end up taking some accounting and some statistics. It should come as no great surprise that these areas also provide you with important tools to put in your decision-making tool kit. In the case of business or government decisions, we get our information from accountants and engineers, organize and compile that information using statistics, and apply the decision rules of economics to choose among the alternative choices.

That's all well and good, but where does the Internet fit into all of this? The Internet is the fastest growing repository of information in the history of the world and is perhaps the largest and most current source of information available to you. There are virtually no subjects about which there is no information. The information contained on the Internet can inform you about current events, provide you with data, and generally help you make better decisions.

However, while the Internet provides great opportunities for finding information, it also presents a couple of problems. First, even though there is a tremendous amount of information available on the Internet, it is in haphazard order, stored in bits and pieces on computers all over the world. While there have been efforts made to organize that information and there are powerful tools available to help search for specific information, you need to know something about where to find the information that interests you. Second, in many cases the information provided on the Internet is not checked by anyone for accuracy. So how do you find information on the Internet and how do you determine its value? Your education, in the broadest sense, will help you with the latter problem. The more you study that which has been sifted and judged worthwhile—whether it's English, history, chemistry, or economics—the better you will be able to "separate the wheat from the chaff."

This book will help you find out how to access the information on the Internet, provide you with some high-quality information sources, and help you use the information you find to your benefit. Specifically, the first two chapters of this book will introduce you to the World Wide Web, show you how to navigate the Internet, and teach you how to find the information you want. The third chapter is more specific and illustrates how to use information from the Internet to help you in your economics courses.

So, back to the original premise. Your instructor expects you to use the Internet for an economics class. Throughout the course remember the basic structure of making choices: gather your information, organize and compile it, and apply your decision rules to make a choice. The Internet is an excellent source of information as well as an outlet for economic research that will allow you to see the tools of economics applied to various problems. This book will help you access that information and give you some tips on how it can be applied in your economics class. Now that you see how the Internet fits into economics, let's get going—there's a whole world of information out there waiting for you!

Where Did the Internet Come From?

We would be remiss if we didn't share at least a little bit of the history of the Internet with you, so here's a very brief overview. The Internet was "born" roughly 25 years ago in an attempt to tie together several existing computer networks used mainly by the government and universities. Originally the notion of networking computers came from the need of the Department of Defense to be able to securely transfer information between the Pentagon and various research sites located around the country. This network (ARPAnet—the Advanced Research Projects Agency network) provided the foundation for not only University-Pentagon communication but University-University communication as well. Soon several additional communication networks developed, each with its own "language," or protocol. The largest and most familiar of these networks are BITNET (Because It's Time NETwork) and EARN (European Area Research Network). Over time these and other networks were connected via "gateways" that made it possible for networks using different protocols to communicate with one another. Eventually, traffic across these networks increased to the point where the gateways were unable to handle the load.

What was needed was a common language that every network "spoke," along with an easy way to navigate and transfer information among widely scattered computers. The recent development of the World Wide Web (WWW) and its underlying communications mechanism has provided this language, or protocol. The World Wide Web has made it easy for even computer novices to access information contained in computers spread out across the world. The ease of accessing (and providing) this information has led to an explosion in the use of this technology. Now, many businesses, schools, and private individuals use the Web daily to transact business, teach courses, and view the latest news. You are on the cutting edge of an exciting new technology that promises to truly transform our lives!

Learning More about the Internet

If you'd like to know more about the history of the Internet—and it's a fascinating story of trial and error, discovery, and flashes of true genius—we recommend the following books and Web sites:

Books:

The Whole Internet: Users Guide and Catalog, Second edition
by Ed Krol O'Reilly and Associates Inc.

Internet Clear & Simple
by Peter McBride Butterworth-Heinemann Publishers

Internet in Plain English
by Bryan Pfaffenberger MIS:Press

World Wide Web Handbook
by Peter Flynn International Thomson Computer Press

World Wide Web Sites:

World Wide Web Consortium
This is a group at MIT that is the focal point for changes, additions, and new uses for the World Wide Web. The Web is not "owned" by anyone, but this organization provides continuity and consistency by overseeing its uses and changes. From here you can go to any of several Web-related sites.

http://www.w3.org/pub/WWW/

Home Page for Tim Berners-Lee, the developer of the Web
This is a biography of the man who started it all from the Particle Physics Laboratory (CERN) in Switzerland.

http://www.w3.org/pub/WWW/People/Berners-Lee-Bio.html/

Netscape's and Microsoft's Home Pages
These are excellent sources for information about the Web and for software to use the Web to its fullest. You can also download the latest version of Netscape Navigator or Internet Explorer (the two most popular Web browsers) from these sites.

http://home.netscape.com/
http://www.microsoft.com/

Chapter 1

Traveling on the Internet

There's a whole world of information on the Internet waiting for you. Those who know how to access this information have a competitive edge over those who don't. This book provides you with the tools necessary to put the Internet to work for you.

As we mentioned in the Introduction, we intend this *Guide* to be interactive, so you should have your computer set up and operational, including the necessary software and an Internet connection. For many of you who are accessing the Internet from a computer lab at a University or College, this will most likely have been done for you already. If you have your own computer, we have summarized in Appendix I the basic resources you will need to connect to the Internet; you should read this information now before continuing.

There are many computers, software packages, and connections that you can use to get onto the Internet. For the most part, however, our examples are based on the Windows95 version of the Netscape Navigator software running on a personal computer. The Netscape software is available for a variety of operating systems, including DOS/Windows, Windows95, Unix, and Macintosh, and is available free of charge to students, educators, and schools. Regardless of the operating system you work on, the "look" of the Netscape software is similar. New versions of this software appear regularly, but they will no doubt include the basic functions we discuss in this manual. Other popular "Web browsers" such as NCSA's Mosaic or Microsoft's Internet Explorer also have many of the same features as Netscape, so what you learn here will be useful when using other Internet browsing software as well.

1.1 How Does the Web Work?

The software that you'll use to access the Internet is commonly called a *Web browser*. Netscape Navigator is an example of a *graphical* Web browser, meaning that it is capable of displaying images in addition to text. Non-graphical browsers that display only text, such as Lynx, are also available, often over a campus computer network. Web browsers function on an information-exchange model called a *Client-Server model* (Figure 1). A *client* (your computer and Web browser software) communicates with a *server* (another computer and Web server software) on the Internet to exchange information. The Internet is made up of thousands of servers around the world, and the Web is a way to connect all the information on these computers. The "web" concept comes from the fact that much of the information is

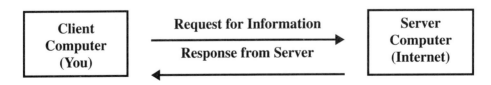

Figure 1. The Client requests information from the server. The requested information is displayed on the client computer.

interconnected (like a spider's web), allowing you to get to particular sources of information in multiple ways. The information that your browser receives from a server is called a *page.*

1.2 Getting Started

So, what do Web pages look like? The best way to answer this is to see for yourself. Sit down in front of a computer and start your Web browser by double-clicking on the left mouse button while the on-screen cursor arrow is positioned over the browser's icon (see Figure 2).

Netscape
Navigator

Figure 2. The Netscape Navigator shortcut icon

Your browser is probably already set to start at a specific page. This start page is often called a *home page.* Unlike a physical page in a book, Web pages may contain sounds and video clips in addition to text and images. In addition, Web pages may extend beyond the borders of your computer screen. Clicking on the left mouse button while the cursor arrow is positioned on the arrows visible along the right (and possibly the bottom) edges of your page will allow you to scroll up and down (or across) the page. From the home page, you can direct the software to look in other locations for information. When you select a particular location, another page of information will be sent to your computer for display.

1.3 How Do I Get to the Party?

As we pointed out, the information on the Internet is literally scattered around the world. In this maze of information, how can you find the information you want? Finding your way around the Internet is really no harder then finding your way to a friend's house. Suppose that your friends are having a party at their new house. If you're familiar with their town, all you need is their address to get to the party. Navigating the Internet with a Web browser is even easier.

Information on the Internet has an "address," just as your friends do. If you already know the Internet address of the information you are seeking, you can type the address and go directly to that information. With Netscape, there are two easy ways to do this:

1. One way is to use your mouse to click on the *Open* toolbar button. (If you don't see a row of toolbar buttons near the top of your Netscape screen, you can make these visible by selecting *Show Toolbar* from the *Options* menu. See Figure 3.) A small window will appear and offer you the opportunity to type in the address of the desired document.

2. Alternately, you can edit the rectangular *Location Bar* located directly under the toolbar buttons. If the Location Bar is not visible, you can open it by selecting *Show Location* from the *Options* menu (see Figure 3 again). The rectangular address window will appear immediately below the toolbar buttons. In this window you will see an Internet address for the current page of information. Position the cursor arrow in the window and click on the left mouse button to edit the address

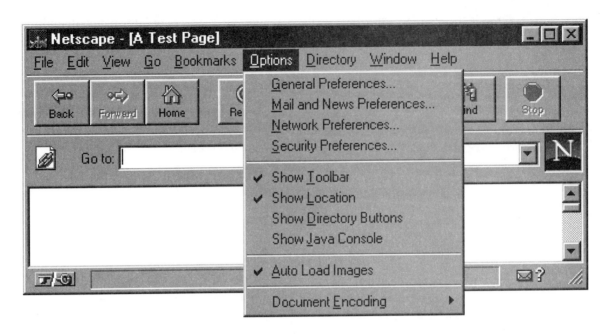

Figure 3. Within Netscape, the selections under the Option menu act as toggle buttons. They can be alternately turned on (with a check mark) or off (without a check mark) by selecting them.

that is showing. Simply delete any part of the address that you don't need and type in the address you're interested in going to. When you start editing the current address the label on the window will change from *Location* to *Go to* (see Figure 4). When you're done typing the new address, hit the return button on your computer and you will be sent to the document at that location.

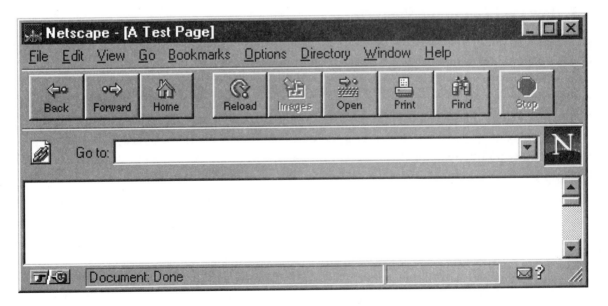

Figure 4. With the *Show Location* and *Show Toolbar* options selected in the *Options* menu, the Netscape menu, toolbar buttons, and location bar are all visible on the screen. You can edit the address that appears in the location bar window. When you begin to do this, the *Location* label changes to a *Go to* label.

Your Turn

To get you started on your Internet journey, we have provided a few addresses for you to try. See where these addresses take you! One word of caution: Be careful when typing the addresses. You need to type them just as they appear, taking notice whether the letters in the address are lower-case or upper-case. Even one incorrect letter or mistyped slash will prevent the browser from finding the correct site. If you make a mistake—and you will sometimes!—just edit the address in the location window and hit the return button again.

http://cnn.com/http://www.whitehouse.gov

http://www.pathfinder.comhttp://www.intellicast.com/

http://ucmp1.berkeley.edu/expo/diapsids/dinosaurs.html

http://www.odci.gov/cia/

1.4 Anatomy of a World Wide Web Address

You've probably seen references to Internet addresses on television commercials, in magazines, or in newspapers. Many companies have created Web pages to advertise and sell their products or simply to provide information. These addresses are called Universal Resource Locators, or URLs for short. Each URL has a couple of basic parts just like a residential address. Internet addresses may seem confusing at first, but think of them as nothing more than postal addresses squished together without any spaces. Let's dissect a URL to give you an idea of how an Internet address is constructed (see Figure 5).

Figure 5.   A typical URL.

The first part of the URL identifies the *protocol* used, or how the information is accessed. In the URL illustrated in Figure 5, "http" refers to the protocol or language that Web servers use to communicate with one another. The colon and slashes are typically used to separate the protocol from the name of the server. The next part of the address usually indicates the name of the institution or company that maintains the server, followed by the *domain* to which the server belongs. Some common domains that you'll see are *.com* for commercial Internet sites, *.edu* for educational institutions, *.org* for organizations, *.mil* for military sites, and *.gov* for government sites. The remainder of the URL indicates the specific location of the Web page on the server.

In your travels, you might jump to a server that is outside your country. Most, but not all, of the information on these servers is in English, despite their foreign location. URLs of foreign servers have an additional section at the end of the server's name. It is a two letter code that denotes the country. Here are a few examples you may encounter on your Internet journeys:

- .au   Australia
- .ca   Canada

- .ch   Switzerland

- .nl   Netherlands

- de   Germany

- .pe   Peru

- uk   United Kingdom

- jp   Japan

- cn   China

- .su   Russia

Your Turn

Try a couple of foreign addresses from the list below. Within seconds you can be connected to a computer across the world!

http://www.jnto.go.jp/
http://www.uni-hamburg.de/index_e.html
http://www.bta.org.uk/
http://www.aaa.com.au/online/aSydney.html

The Internet began with a text-based format, and some servers still provide information in this format. Browsers can also access these types of documents. Try the following URLs, and notice how the presentation differs from those you viewed earlier.

ftp://oak.oakland.edu/pub/
gopher://gopher.micro.umn.edu:70/1

1.5 Navigating the WWW Using Hyperlinks

The problem with typing in the location of Web pages is that you need to know the URL of the site you're interested in. The whole point of the Web is to make it easy to get to information on the Internet *without* having to know a lot of computer jargon. One of the best features of the Web is that you can access (navigate) pages through the use of *hyperlinks*. These hyperlinks have been created by the author of a page to make accessing Internet information easier. Rather than remembering URLs you can simply scroll through a page and use your mouse to navigate the Web. Hyperlinks are usually indicated by colored or underlined words on a page, or possibly as images. In the case of image-based hyperlinks, a single image may contain multiple hyperlinks. You'll know you're at a hyperlink on a page when you move the cursor arrow over a word or image and the cursor turns into a hand. In addition, the address that the hyperlink points to will appear at the bottom of the Netscape screen. Clicking on the left button of the mouse while the cursor is positioned on a hyperlink will take you to the specified location on the Internet.

Your Turn

The easiest way to start your Internet journey is to begin with a directory that someone else has constructed. These directories are simply lists of hyperlinks, arranged by subject. Try one of the following popular Internet directories and follow the provided hyperlinks on an Internet adventure! Where do your travels take you?

http://www.yahoo.com/
http://www.einet.net/

1.6 How Can I Get Back Home?

Like Dorothy in the Wizard of Oz, your travels on the Internet may have taken you far from where you started. Rather than clicking your heels to return home, however, you can get back to where you came from with a few clicks of your mouse. On the Internet you're never far from home.

Back and Forward Button. The *Back* and *Forward* buttons are located on the Netscape toolbar that appears at the top of the screen just below the menu headings (see Figure 6). Clicking the left mouse button while the cursor arrow is positioned over the *Back* button will take you to the last page you accessed. Clicking on the *Back* button again will take you back another page, and so on. You can go back and forth through the pages you've visited—one page at a time—by using the *Back* and *Forward* buttons repeatedly. In other words, Netscape leaves a trail of crumbs for you as you go on your journey.

Figure 6. The Netscape Navigator Web browser offers a wide selection of basic navigation and control options. The navigation tools can be accessed using the menu choices or the toolbar buttons. Other browsers have toolbars with similar functions.

Go Menu Option. If you've been working along with your manual and your browser at the same time, you've probably been to many places on the Web. As we just mentioned, you can move back and forth between your selections by using the *Forward* and *Back* buttons on the browser's toolbar. But what do you do if you want to go back to a site you visited fifteen jumps ago? Well, Netscape allows you to jump *directly* to any of the places you've visited on your current Internet journey. Simply click on the *GO* menu option to bring up a list of these locations, arranged by order of visit. By positioning the cursor arrow over a specific location on this list and clicking the left mouse button, you'll be sent there directly, without having to use the *Back* button over and over.

Home Button. If you get tired of traveling the Internet and want to get back to your original home page, there's a quick and easy way to do it using Netscape. Clicking on the *Home* button located on the

Netscape toolbar will bring you back to where you started your Internet journey, whether it's Kansas or somewhere else.

1.7 Remembering Where You've Been: Bookmarks

O.K., let's say you've found a really interesting page on the Internet. How can you find that page tomorrow or next week? You *could* write down the URL and type it in the next time you want to visit that page, but there's a better way. You can save a *bookmark* to this page that will allow you to return to the page with just a couple clicks of your mouse. Think of it as your own personal index of interesting places on the Internet. If you're working on your own computer you can create a bookmark by selecting *Add Bookmark* from the *Bookmarks* menu on your browser (see Figure 7). This will create a file on the hard drive of your computer with the page's title and address in it.

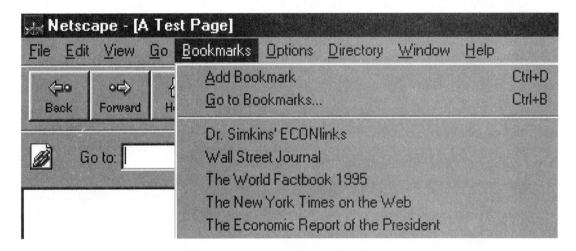

Figure 7. After you've added bookmarks to your browser, they will appear in a list under the *Bookmarks* menu on the menubar. Once you've selected a list of bookmarks you may view them and organize them into categories. You can also open the *Bookmarks* window using the *Window* menu.

If you're working on a computer in a University computer lab, chances are that you won't be able to save files to the hard drive of the machine you're working on, or if you can, it's likely that they won't be there when you come back. You can still save your bookmarks to a file, but you'll need to save them on a floppy disk. To create a bookmark file, click on the *Bookmarks* menu button and select *Go to Bookmarks*. This will open up a *bookmark window* with a new set of menus. In the *bookmark window*, select *File* and then choose *Save as*. Now insert your floppy disk and type in the full pathname of the file you want to save your bookmarks in (for example, a:\bookmark.htm). Netscape will then use this file to save any bookmarks you add to your list during your Netscape session. One piece of advice: Before you are done with your Netscape session, make sure to go back to the *Bookmarks* window and save your updated bookmark file. You can share your bookmark file with others or use it the next time you come to the computer lab. Just remember that if you're saving your bookmarks on a floppy disk, you'll need to tell Netscape the location of your bookmark file at the start of each session if you want to access your existing bookmarks or save any new ones.

Now if you use your mouse to go back to the Bookmarks menu, you'll see that your favorite site is just a click away. You don't have to memorize the URL, and you don't have to haphazardly jump around until you find it again.

1.8 Some Helpful Tips

Reloading Pages. A useful Netscape tool is the *Reload* toolbar button (see Figure 6). If a page does not transfer properly, you can click on the *Reload* button to reload the information you are requesting. This is particularly helpful if the page you are accessing is updated frequently.

Stopping the Flow of Information. Sometimes you'll find that a page seems to take forever to display on your screen, possibly because of slow Internet connection or heavy Internet traffic. If you get tired of waiting, you can click on the *Stop* menu button to stop the incoming flow of information (see Figure 6). There is an icon in the upper right-hand corner of the Netscape screen that displays motion (shooting stars) when information is being transferred from the server to your computer screen. The motion will stop when all the information has been transferred or when you click on the *Stop* button.

Turning off Image Loading. While Web pages filled with graphics may look nice, the tradeoff is that they may take a long time to appear on your computer screen, especially if you are using a modem to access the Internet. You can speed up access to Web pages by turning off automatic image-loading in Netscape. To do this, click on the *Options* menu button and then click on the *Auto Load Images* line (see Figure 3). Notice that this line functions as a toggle switch, with the checkmark appearing when the option is turned on. From that point on Netscape will load only the *text* that appears on the Web pages you visit. When you find a place of interest you can view the graphics by clicking the *Auto Load Image* line again and reloading the page.

Using Helper Applications. Most of the information on Web pages, such as text and images, can be interpreted directly by Web browsers. In recent years, however, Web site developers have been adding more complicated material to their Web pages, such as music, live audio broadcasts, videos, and three-dimensional "virtual reality" environments. Still other pages may include links to specially formatted documents, such as those generated by a word processor, that Netscape can't process.

While each succeeding generation of Web browsers includes more software "plug-ins," which work seamlessly with the browser to interpret these special files, from time to time you will travel to Web pages that contain links to material that require additional software to view, activate, or listen to. If Netscape cannot directly process the information on a page, it will provide you with three options: (1) find a "helper application" that is capable of processing this information, (2) save the information to a file on your computer for you to access later using the required software, or (3) return back to the page you last accessed.

"Helper applications" are software programs you must purchase or download and install on your computer before Netscape can access them. In many cases where specially formatted material is included on a Web page, the author also includes a hyperlink to a site that contains a downloadable version of the software necessary for viewing that file. After downloading and installing the software on your computer (follow the directions at the download site) you can use the browser software to launch this program whenever you run across a file of this type. When Netscape prompts you for action, simply select the "find helper application" option and indicate the location of the software on your computer. The helper application will start up and present the material in the file. Alternately, you can save the file to a disk and use the helper application directly to view the material contained there.

Conserving Disk Space. The browser keeps a temporary copy of frequently accessed Web pages on your computer, allowing you to quickly return to sites you have visited during your session without having to reconnect to the actual site. These temporary files are supposed to be deleted at the end of your browsing session, but they can take up valuable disk space even while you're browsing. To remove these files from your computer, click on the *Options* menu toolbar and click on "Network Preferences" (see Figure 3). Next, select the *Cache* menu tab and click on the *Clear Disk Cache Now* button.

Customizing Browser Appearance. Using Netscape, under the *Options* menu you can make several choices to further customize the appearance and function of the browser. Most of these options are listed under the *General Preferences* submenu (see Figure 3) and give you control over such features such as the default home page location, font colors and sizes, and the appearance of your hyperlinks (notice that they change color after you've visited a site). Feel free to play with these options until you get the results you like. Netscape will save your settings when you click on the "OK" button at the bottom of the page. If you're working in a university computer lab, however, remember that you may not be able to change these settings or, if you can, that they may disappear after your session. In this case, it's probably best to use the browser as it was configured by the computing center.

1.9 Help is Only a Click Away

Netscape and other browser software include extensive on-line information to assist you in using the browser software and navigating the Internet. Simply click on *Help* (see Figure 6) at any time to access this information. Netscape provides an on-line Handbook and a list of frequently asked questions and their answers, in addition to other resources. Think of this as your own personal roadside assistance plan as you travel the Internet.

Your Turn

Now that you've got the hang of it, give the following URLs a try. Where else do they lead you?

> *http://espnet.sportszone.com/*
> *http://www.foxnetwork.com/*
> *http://www.mtv.com/index.html*
> *http://www.msnbc.com/*
> *http://www.microsoft.com/automap/*

When you find something that you think is fun and interesting, save it or give it to a friend.

If you're feeling adventurous, try the following address. This site will randomly place you somewhere on the Internet. You will experience many different places and discover some that have value to you. If you find something that you like, set a bookmark or record the URL so that you can easily return to it in the future.

> *http://www.netcreations.com/magicurl/index.html*

1.10 A Final Word about Navigating on the Internet

Remember that the Internet is a dynamic environment that is becoming increasingly popular and is constantly changing. Information accessed by hyperlinks may suddenly disappear or may change locations. Occasionally you may get a Netscape message indicating that the requested information could not be located or that the server is busy. When this happens, don't get discouraged. Try the URL again later or look for an alternative source for the information. Remember, you're on the cutting edge of a new technology and there are going to be some bumps along the way. Even so, the journey is well worth it.

Chapter 2

Finding Information on the Internet

We pointed out in the introduction that there are a couple of problems associated with the Internet. First, information on the Internet is scattered all over the world on computers run by government agencies, academic institutions, commercial service providers, and home computer users. Second, the accuracy of this information is generally not checked by anyone other than the person who makes it available on a server.

How to determine what is worthwhile is beyond the scope of this book, but how to find the information you need is a skill we can help you develop. Finding something on the Web is much like a game of hide-and-seek or a scavenger hunt; if you are systematic about your searching, the odds of being successful increase greatly. There are a number of methods for locating information on the Internet. First (and sometimes the most interesting) is pure blind luck! You happen to follow a hyperlink from one document to another and *voila!,* there it is— exactly what you needed. You might also follow a friend's suggestion, such as "I found that at http://www....", or use a Web address you saw advertised on television or in a magazine. However, the Internet provides much more efficient and powerful ways of tracking down information—directories and search engines. It pays to understand these tools; they can save you hours of aimless wandering on the Internet.

2.1 Using Directories to Find Information

General Directories. The first of these search tools involves using a *directory index.* Using a directory is much like using the Yellow Pages in your telephone book to locate a local restaurant or a 24-hour copy center. You simply begin looking by category and narrow your categories down until you find what you want. Internet directories and the Yellow Pages generally index information by topic, with specific addresses listed under those topics.

While these comprehensive directories are wonderful if you are just browsing or spending the afternoon searching for that flash of insight that will guarantee you an "A" on your next paper, sometimes you need information for your economics class and you need it NOW! (Class in ten minutes!) In that case, having access to a more specific directory geared toward economics is preferable.

Economics Directories. Economics directories typically consist of a page of economics-related hyperlinks maintained by someone as part of their Web site. Generally these are fairly specialized and you need to know where they are located to use them. As an example, take a look at a couple of economics directories we have created:

> *http://www.elon.edu/users/o/econ/links/*
> *http://aurora.ncat.edu/~simkinss/econlinks.html*

Probably the most comprehensive index of economic information on the Web is Bill Goffe's *Resources for Economists on the Internet.* This guide is located at

> *http://econwpa.wustl.edu/EconFAQ/EconFAQ.html*

There is also a Web site that has been created to support your textbook. This site contains links to current events stories and additional economic information related to the material in your textbook. To access this information, take a look at

http://www.prenhall.com/phlip

Your Turn

We've created an assignment to give you some practice using Internet directories. Let's say you are assigned to find out about current and past employment conditions in a state of your choosing. Because your Aunt Tillie lives in Salt Lake City, you choose to explore Utah. Let's do the assignment in a couple of ways. First let's take a journey through a couple of Internet directories such as Yahoo and EINET Galaxy. Start with Yahoo's Internet directory.

- Go to Yahoo at *http://www.yahoo.com/*
- Now, follow the directory links to find information on current unemployment rates in Utah.
- First choose Government by clicking on the highlighted word, then choose U.S. States.
- Choose Utah, then select Department of Employment Security.

You should now be at a page which looks something like:

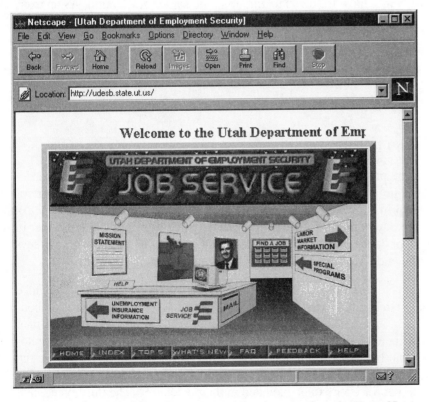

Figure 8. This is the Utah Department of Employment Security Page. Note that this is an excellent example of an *image map*. An image map is a hyperlink that uses the location of the cursor on the screen to determine the URL for the jump.

15

- Click on the "Labor Market Information" sign on the wall and you should find the non-agricultural employment for Utah.

Now complete the assignment using Galaxy's EINET directory:

- First connect to EINET at *http://www.einet.net/*
- Now follow the directory links through Government to find the non-agricultural employment for Utah.
- First select Government from the list of topics. From the Directories select Government Sites and Databases.
- Select World, U.S. Federal and State Bodies and Agencies, then select State Government on the Net and follow the State & Local Government on the Net.
- Select Utah, and then select Department of Employment Security.

There you are, at the same location you reached via the Yahoo directory path.

As a second approach, try a search engine. Go to MetaCrawler (*http://www.metacrawler.com*) and enter *Utah Employment Security* in the keyword box and select the *all* radio button. When you click on *go,* the listing of sites with Utah Employment Security in them will be returned to you. Select the Department of Employment Security and, again, there you are.

There are several other paths you might have followed to end up at the same information. As an exercise, go back to the home page for Galaxy (*http://www.einet.net/*) and follow a different path to locate the same information.

Hint: Click on G̲o from the header bar at the top of your screen and select Galaxy to go back in one jump.

2.2 Using Search Engines to Find Information

Your choices in using a directory are pretty broad. Unfortunately, however, you may not have a particular category in mind when you begin your search. You may be in a situation where you need more of a "shotgun" approach. The other primary method of finding information on the Internet is to use a *search engine.* A search engine is particularly useful when you need to find information that is either in a category you are unfamiliar with or does not lend itself to categorization. Search engines come in several varieties, and to use them efficiently you should understand the various ways they work.

Search engines are among the most helpful tools available to you on the Internet. Essentially they take the *keywords* that you type in and search a database for the URLs of sites that have those words embedded in them. Search engines can be divided into three basic categories: (1) passive, (2) active, and (3) meta engines. The first type includes those engines, like the one that works with the *Yahoo!* directory, which have only information that has been submitted to the database for inclusion. These are the *passive* engines. *Active* search engines, such as Lycos, employ a bit of computer code called a *worm* or a *spider* to actively search the Internet for URLs to be included in their databases. The third type, *meta engines* like MetaCrawler, do not maintain a database at all, but submit keywords to several search engines and then collate the results.

Each type of search engine has its advantages and disadvantages. Passive engines are limited to the amount of information stored in their database. The tradeoff is that the information has been checked for accuracy and for the quality of the Web site. These search engines are the most labor intensive to maintain, but are generally the most dependable. Active engines maintain a database of the entire Web, but the sites may be temporary, mislabeled, or filled with junk. These generate a great number of "hits" (that is, they find many URLs containing your keywords) but you must then sort through the resulting list to determine which sites are most useful. Meta engines, in effect, run searches on several engines at once, saving you the effort of multiple searches. However, most search engines return hits in sets of ten, and only the first set of hits will be included in the meta engine's resulting list of URLs. Thus, if the site you want happens to be the thirtieth one listed on every search engine, a meta engine search will not uncover it.

A few engines are worthy of note:

Yahoo!. The Yahoo (*http://www.yahoo.com*) search engine can search either a particular sub-category of the Yahoo directory or the entire directory. Thus it tends to be a pretty efficient engine, since Yahoo is a large, comprehensive, directory.

Webcrawler. The WebCrawler (*http://www.webcrawler.com*) is another comprehensive search engine, fast and generally efficient.

Lycos. Lycos (*http://www.lycos.com*) is perhaps the most comprehensive of the group. The folks at Lycos advertise themselves as cataloging *all* the Web, and they certainly come close.

Alta Vista. If you are willing to have a huge number of hits try AltaVista (*http://www.altavista.com*). This active engine not only maintains a database of the keywords identified by the maintainers of each site, it keeps a record of all the words on the first page of each site it visits. Thus, if there is an Internet site dealing with blowfish and it mentions that they fill themselves with gas, this search engine will likely find that site when you are searching for information on "gas powered model airplanes." This can be a bit of a pain, but it is worth the extra effort when you are looking for something obscure.

MetaCrawler. One of the better meta-engines is MetaCrawler (http://www.metacrawler.com). This search meta-engine submits your keywords to several different search engines: Yahoo!, Excite, Galaxy, Lycos, WebCrawler, Inktomi, and others. Then it collates the results and returns a list of URLs that (as nearly as possible) has each site included only once.

With a little practice, and with several search engines included in your bookmark file, you can become quite proficient at finding things quickly.

Your Turn

It's homework time again, and this time your professor has asked you to find information on sock manufacturing. You could use a directory and follow the links—from business, to textiles, to knitting, to socks—and perhaps you would find useful information. Alternatively, you could submit a request to a search engine and hope to turn up something using the keywords "socks" or "hosiery." Try the search engine approach, and to broaden your search as much as possible, use both an active engine and a meta-engine.

2.3 Saving What You Have Found

Whether you use a search engine or a directory to find your information, or simply stumble across what you need, turning in your assignment in the form *"Dr. Jones, if you go to **http://www.here.is.the.stuff/ I/hope/it/works you'll find the material that can be used to answer last night's assignment"*** probably will not endear you to your professor. You need to take the material and include it in your report, and if your memory is normal, you will not be able to simply recall all the pertinent information as you write up your assignment. There are several ways of saving information you have found on the Internet: (1) you can save it to disk (both images and text), (2) cut and paste it into another document, or (3) print it. Additionally you can e-mail a document to anyone you wish.

Saving to Disk

To save a Web page to disk you simply click on the *File* menu button and select the *Save As* option (see Figures 9 and 10). Next, type in the full pathname of where you wish to save the document (for example, *a:\savethis.txt*) and press *Enter.* You will usually be saving to a floppy disk in the A drive. However you may be saving to a hard drive if you are at home and not in a university computer lab. The example illustrates saving to a floppy.

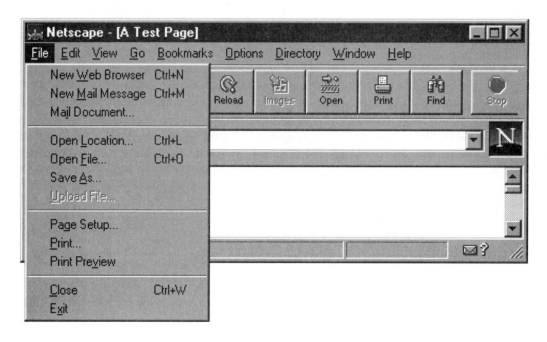

Figure 9.   Clicking on the *File* menu button opens a drop-down menu. From this menu you can save a Web page to disk, e-mail the page to someone, or print the page.

E-Mailing a Web Page

Note: Before you attempt to use e-mail from within Netscape, be sure that the program is set up to send and receive e-mail. How to go about setting up Netscape to handle e-mail is covered in Appendix II.

To send a Web page to someone using e-mail, simply click on the *File* menu button and select *Mail Document.* A new window will open into which you insert the e-mail address of the recipient, the subject of the e-mail, the address of anyone you wish to send a copy to, and the text of any message you

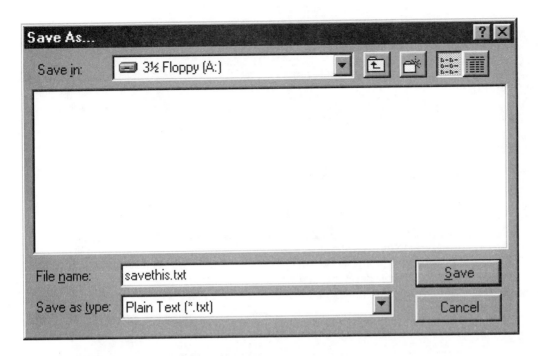

Figure 10. Clicking on *Save As* from the drop-down menu will open the "dialogue box" shown here. In this example you are saving a file named *savethis.txt* to a floppy disk in the A drive.

wish to accompany the document—such as "HEY LINDA, I FOUND THE ANSWER TO TO-NIGHT'S HOMEWORK!!!!" (see Figure 11). The Web page will be attached to the message and both will be sent as soon as you click the *Send* button.

Printing a Web Page

This is the easiest way to save your information and gives you a hard copy of the Web page you have found. Click on the *File* menu button and select *Print*. The Print dialogue box will open (See Figure 12). The default is to print the entire contents of the Web page, but you can choose to print less than this if you like. After making sure you have the correct printer selected and paper loaded in the printer, select OK. You can also use the *Print* toolbar button to access the Print dialogue box.

Cutting, Copying, and Pasting Web Information

You can cut or copy and paste from Netscape just as you would from any other Windows-based software. Select the portion of the Web page you wish to copy or cut by holding the left mouse-button and dragging the cursor over the relevant material on the Web page. Next, either select *Cut* or *Copy* from the *Edit* drop-down menu or press Crtl+X (to cut) or Crtl+C (to copy). Then change your active window to your word processor or other software, position the insertion point (the vertical bar) where you wish the Web page information to be placed, and select *Paste* from the *Edit* drop-down menu, or press Ctrl+V to paste the information from the clipboard to the document.

Saving Images from Web Pages

To save an image such as a photo or graphic from the Web you must save it as a separate file from the text. The most efficient way to accomplish this is to position the cursor on the image and click the *right*

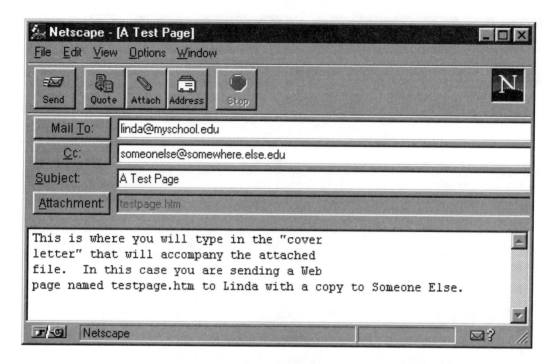

Figure 11. Clicking on *Mail Document* from the *File* menu will open the window shown above. You will need to enter the e-mail address of the principal recipient, anyone you wish to send a copy to, and the body of any message you wish to send along. The Subject will be the title of the Web page (in this case "A Test Page") but can be modified by simply clicking in the *Subject* box and editing the contents. Pressing the *Send* button will send the message and the attached Web page to the addresses indicated.

mouse button. A *Save This Image As* dialogue box will open, similar to the box in Figure 10. The filename defaults to the name of the image file on the Web page, but you may change it to whatever you wish. The extension of an image filename (.gif, .jpg, and so on) lets the computer know the file type so that it can be viewed properly, so it is best to leave the filename extension alone. Whatever you name the file, you must give the full path of the location where you want the file to be saved. Again, in most cases that will be on a floppy disk in the A drive.

You now know how to get Netscape up and running, search for information, and save the information that you find. So far so good. The next chapter deals with the information that is available to you on the Web as it relates to your economics class.

Your Turn

As an exercise in saving and printing information from the Web, go to Chapter 3 and use this skill to create your own Web home page on disk. There is a template located at *http://www.prenhall.com/econsurfing/student.htm* which has been created just for this purpose. Simply download the file and save it on a floppy disk (or on your computer) with the name *student.htm*. You can then view the Web page in Netscape and use the included hyperlinks.

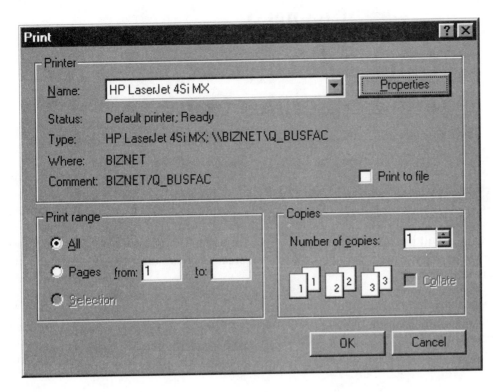

Figure 12.   Clicking on *Print* in the *File* drop-down menu or clicking the *Print* toolbar button will open the Printdialogue box. From the *Setup* button you may select your printer and other options. Clicking on **OK** will initiate the printing.

To view the file in Netscape after you have saved it, simply click the *File* menu button and select the *Open File* option. Enter the full pathname of the saved file (for example, *a:/student.htm*) in the resulting dialogue box and click *Open.* The Web page should appear on your Netscape screen. Chapter 3 provides additional information on how to customize this Web page according to your personal interests.

Chapter 3

Using The Internet in Your Economics Course

Now that you have some practice navigating the Internet, it's time to start putting this information resource to work for you in your economics course. In this chapter we'll provide you with the addresses of a number of Web sites that we think provide useful information for a wide variety of economics courses. When compiling this list we avoided the temptation to be encyclopedic. The result is a list of economics resources that will provide you with a rich set of information without overwhelming you. When you find Web sites that are particularly useful to you, create a bookmark file so that you can return to them quickly in the future.

It is important to note that learning economics requires you to *process* the information you obtain, so we also want to show you how you can use economic information to help you broaden and deepen your understanding of economics. To aid you in this endeavor we have included in this chapter a sample economics assignment, along with some additional ideas about how you might use the Internet in your economics course.

3.1 Sources of Economic Information

As we mentioned, one of the problems associated with using the Internet is knowing where to look for the information you are seeking. In the last chapter we focused on two methods for locating information on the Internet: directories and search engines. In this section we'll point you to specific sources of economic information, ranging from broad economic directories to sites containing current economic statistics.

Note: Because the Web is dynamic, Web sites sometimes change, or worse yet, disappear altogether. The sites selected in the remainder of this chapter were accurate when this Guide *was written.*

Indexes of Economic Information

There are a number of comprehensive directories or indexes of economic information available on the Internet. One of them we mentioned in the last chapter, Bill Goffe's *Guide to Economic Information on the Internet.* This is the most comprehensive source for economic information on the Internet and is updated regularly. In addition to addresses of specific sites there are also descriptions of what you'll find there.

Guide to Economic Information on the Internet
   http://econwpa.wustl.edu/ EconFAQ/EconFAQ.html

There are a number of Internet directories that provide broad coverage of economics and business information. These tend to be encyclopedic, but some include a search engine to help you narrow the focus of your search. A representative sample is given below.

YAHOO
http://www.yahoo.com
Einet
http://einet.net/galaxy/Social-Sciences.html
Library of Congress
gopher://marvel.loc.gov:70/11/global/econ/econ
Infoseek
http://www.infoseek.com

A number of universities also maintain directories of economic information. Check out the following sites for extensive lists of economics resources.

Sam Houston State Univ.
gopher://Niord.SHSU.edu:70/11gopher_root:[_DATA. ECONOMICS]
Rutgers University
http://www.libraries.rutgers.edu/rulib/socsci/econ/econ.html
Washington Univ.-St. Louis
gopher://wuecon.wustl.edu:671/1
Rice University
http://riceinfo.rice.edu/Internet/

Economics and Finance-Related Indexes

The following index provides a comprehensive source of economics and finance-related information.

KiwiClub Web
http://kiwiclub.bus.utexas.edu/

Current National and International News

Read late-breaking news releases on a full range of topics by visiting the following news sites. Content on these sites is continually updated, so you'll be on top of the latest news. Many of the sites have specific sections devoted to economic and financial news, along with links to related information.

National Newspapers

The New York Times
http://www.nytimes.com/
Washington Post
http://www.washingtonpost.com/
Los Angeles Times
http://www.latimes.com/
USA Today
http://www.usatoday.com/

Other News Media

CNN
http://www.cnn.com/

MSNBC

http://www.msnbc.com

Pathfinder

http://pathfinder.com/

Online U.S. News

http://www.usnews.com/usnews/main.htm

National Public Radio

http://www.npr.org

ABC Internet Hourly News

http://www.real.com/contentp/abc24/ihn.html

Reuters News Service

http://www.reuters.com/news/

Current Business News

Keep current with up-to-the minute economic, business, and financial news. A number of on-line news providers post business news on the Internet as it unfolds, continually updating the information throughout the day. Many of these sites also provide links to current financial market conditions, such as stock indexes, interest rates, and exchange rates, as well as industry-specific information. Use this information to bring real world examples to your classroom discussion.

CNN Financial

http://www.cnnfn.com/index.html

The Wall Street Journal

http://wsj.com/

MSNBC-Commerce

http://www.msnbc.com/news/COM_Front.asp

New York Times/Business

http://www.nytimes.com/yr/mo/day/business/

Washington Post/Business

http://washingtonpost.com/ wp-srv/business/front.htm

Los Angeles Times/Business

http://www.latimes.com/HOME/BUSINESS/

Bloomberg's Business News

http://www.bloomberg.com/

USA Today Money

http://www.usatoday.com/money/mfront.html

Daily Financial Market and Business Reports

Microsoft Investor

http://investor.msn.com/Contents.Asp

FORTUNE Business Report

http://pathfinder.com/fortune/fbr/

MONEY Daily

http://pathfinder.com/money/moneydaily/latest/

Current Economic Indicators

The full press releases of important economic statistics are available on-line, usually the day they are released. Check out the news behind the headlines and keep up to date with current economic conditions in the economy. The Federal Reserve's *Beige Book* provides a region-by-region summary of economic conditions, updated about every six weeks.

The Federal Reserve's Beige Book
  http://www.bog.frb.fed.us/fomc/bb/current/
Economic Statistics Briefing Room
  http://www.whitehouse.gov/fsbr/esbr.html
BLS Economy at a Glance
  http://stats.bls.gov:80/eag.table.html

Current Economic Statistics
Gross Domestic Product BEA News Releases
  http://www.bea.doc.gov/bea/newsinf.html
Tables
  http://www.bea.doc.gov/bea/niptbl-d.html

Employment
BLS News Release
  http://stats.bls.gov/news.release/empsit.nws.htm

Consumer Prices/Inflation
BLS News Release
  http://stats.bls.gov/news.release/cpi.nws.htm

Interest Rates
Federal Reserve
  http://www.bog.frb.fed.us/releases/H15/Current/
NY Fed. Res. Bank
  http://www.ny.frb.org/pihome/mktrates/dlyrates/

Exchange Rates
NY Fed. Res. Bank
  http://www.ny.frb.org/pihome/mktrates/forex12.shtml

Current Financial Market Information

These sites provide direct links to current financial market information such as interest rates, exchange rates, stock market indexes, mutual fund indexes, and individual stock and mutual fund quotes. These are continually updated so you can keep track of important financial information throughout the day.

CNN Financial
  http://www.cnnfn.com/markets/us_markets.html
Bloomberg
  http://www.bloomberg.com/welcome.html

USA Today Market Scoreboard
http://www.usatoday.com/money/msfront.html
NetWorth
http://networth.galt.com/
Microsoft Investor
http://investor.msn.com/contents.asp

Economic Analysis and Forecasts

The Bank of America provides weekly economic analyses and forecasts on-line. If you want to get a summary of what's happening in the U.S. and international economy, as well as a short-term forecast of future economic conditions, check out these sites.

Weekly U.S. Economic Briefing
http://www.bankamerica.com/capmkt/brief_us.html
Weekly International Economic Briefing
http://www.bankamerica.com/capmkt/brief_intl.html
Exchange Rate Forecasts
http://www.bankamerica.com/econ_indicator/foreignov.html
U.S. Economic Forecasts
http://www.bankamerica.com/econ_indicator/wall_econ.html

Economic Policy Analysis

Economic policy institutes carry out economic research on public policy issues that are suitable for classroom discussions and paper topics. In some cases the institutes have a conservative or liberal viewpoint, while others claim to be bipartisan. This is a great place to supplement the economic theory presented in your textbook with real-world applications. See what economics has to say about public policy issues in our country.

Electronic Policy Network
http://www.epn.org/
Policy Briefs from the Brookings Institute
http://www.brook.edu/es/policy/policy.htm
Economic Policy Institute
http://epinet.org/
The Jerome Levy Economics Institute of Bard College
http://epn.org//levy.html
Cato Institute
http://www.cato.org/
The Heritage Foundation
http://www.heritage.org/
Progressive Policy Institute
http://www.dlcppi.org/
The American Prospect
http://epn.org/prospect.html

U.S. Economic and Financial Data

If you have a research project or assignment that requires U.S. economic data, here are a few places to look. Some of the sites provide graphs as well as numbers.

Econ Data and Links
http://www.csufresno.edu/Economics/econ_EDL.htm
Economic Time Series Page
http://bos.business.uab.edu/data/data.htm
Bureau of Labor Statistics
http://stats.bls.gov:80/top20.html
Federal Reserve Economic Data
http://www.stls.frb.org/fred/
Regional Economic Information
http://www.lib.virginia.edu/socsci/reis/reis1.html
Census Bureau Statistics
http://www.census.gov/
Statistical Abstract Of the U.S.
http://www.census.gov/stat_abstract/
USDA Economic Statistics
http://usda.mannlib.cornell.edu/usda/usda.html
County and City Databook
http://www.lib.virginia.edu/socsci/ccdb/

International Economic and Financial Data

There are a number of sites that provide international economic data. Some of the sites provide country-specific information on social and economic conditions in addition to economic statistics.

Penn World Tables
http://cansim.epas.utoronto.ca:5680/pwt/pwt.html
CIA World Fact Book
http://www.odci.gov/cia/publications/nsolo/wfb-all.htm
Statistics Canada
http://www.statcan.ca/start.html
Deutsche Bundesbank
http://www.bundesbank.de/index_e.html
Bank of Japan
http://www.boj.go.jp/en/index.htm
Banque de France
http://www.banque-france.fr/us/home.htm
The Bank of Canada
http://www.bank-banque-canada.ca/english/intro-e.htm
The Bank of England
http://www.bankofengland.co.uk/

Money and Banking Resources

If you have questions about the Federal Reserve, the banking system, or monetary policy, this is the place to look! The Federal Reserve System provides an extensive array of macroeconomic information and data on its Internet sites. Many of the regional Federal Reserve banks provide on-line publications exploring current economic and financial issues, as well as links to summaries of current economic conditions, current and historical economic statistics, and public-information documents relating to money, banking, and financial markets.

Board of Governors of the Federal Reserve System
http://www.bog.frb.fed.us/
Mark Bernkopf's Central Banking Resource Center
http://patriot.net/~bernkopf/

Federal Reserve Banks and Monetary Policy

Atlanta
http://www.frbatlanta.org/
Boston
http://www.std.com/frbbos/
Chicago
http://www.frbchi.org/
Cleveland
http://www.clev.frb.org/
Dallas
http://www.dallasfed.org/
Kansas City
http://www.kc.frb.org/
Minneapolis
http://woodrow.mpls.frb.fed.us/
New York
http://www.ny.frb.org/
Philadelphia
http://www.phil.frb.org/
Richmond
http://www.rich.frb.org/
St. Louis
http://www.stls.frb.org/
San Francisco
http://www.frbsf.org/

Foreign Central Banks

Deutsche Bundesbank
http://www.bundesbank.de/index_e.html
Bank of Japan
http://www.boj.go.jp/en/index.htm
Banque de France
http://www.banque-france.fr/us/home.htm
The Bank of Canada
http://www.bank-banque-canada.ca/
english/intro-e.htm

The Bank of England
http://www.bankofengland.co.uk/

Economics and Business Related Magazines

You'll find an increasing number of magazines publishing on-line, including the most popular business periodicals. These are a great source of current-events articles; use them to apply economic concepts to real-world events. Many on-line magazines include only a selection of articles but give you the opportunity to search the contents of current and back issues.

Fortune
http://www.pathfinder.com/fortune/
Business Week
http://www.businessweek.com/
Forbes
http://www.forbes.com/
The Economist
http://www.economist.com/

U.S. Government Agencies and Other Government Sites

U.S. government agencies are the primary providers of most economic and social statistics. You can gain direct access to these agencies using the sites listed below. Many of these agencies publish a broad range of useful government documents on-line.

Library of Congress-Explore The Internet
http://lcweb.loc.gov/global/explore.html
Government Information Locator
http://info.er.usgs.gov/gils/index.html
The White House
http://www.whitehouse.gov/WH/Welcome.html
THOMAS Legislative Info.
http://thomas.loc.gov/
Department of the Treasury
http://www.ustreas.gov/
Social Security Administration
http://www.ssa.gov/SSA_Home.html
Internal Revenue Service
http://www.irs.ustreas.gov/prod/
Bureau of Economic Analysis
http://www.bea.doc.gov/
Bureau of Labor Statistics
http://stats.bls.gov/
Census Bureau
http://www.census.gov/
Federal Deposit Insurance Corporation
http://www.fdic.gov/

U.S. Government Documents

There are a number of U.S. government documents that are particularly useful for economics students. A few of these are listed below. The annual *Economic Report of the President* includes in-depth discussions of microeconomic and macroeconomic policy issues as well as an extensive database of U.S. (and some international) macroeconomic data.

Economic Report of the President
http://www.access.gpo.gov/eop/
U.S. Budget Information
http://www.access.gpo.gov/omb/omb003.html
U.S. Industrial Outlook
http://www.ita.doc.gov/industry/otea/usio/usio95.html
U.S. Occupational Outlook Handbook
gopher://gopher.umsl.edu/11/library/govdocs/ooha
North American Free Trade Agreement
http://www.whitehouse.gov/WH/Publications/html/nafta.html
General Agreements on Tariffs and Trade
http://trading.wmw.com/gatt/

International Economic Organizations

Check out these international organizations for press releases, economic analysis, and public policy discussions.

United Nations
http://www.unsystem.org/
World Bank
http://www.worldbank.org/html/Welcome.html
World Trade Organization
http://www.wto.org/Welcome.html
European Union
http://europa.eu.int
OECD
http://www.oecd.org/
G7 Information
http://utl1.library.utoronto.ca/www/g7/index.html

Law and Economics Resources

The Internet sites listed below provide a good starting point for investigating the relationship between law and economics. Many of the sites provide extensive links to other law and economics resources.

The Law and Economic Sites
http://www-leland.stanford.edu/~tstanley/lawecon.html
Antitrust Policy
http://www.antitrust.org/
RISKWeb
http://www.riskweb.com/
SEC Edgar Database
http://www.sec.gov/edgarhp.htm

Your Turn

Here's an exercise to get you exploring economics-related Internet sites.

Go to the Federal Reserve's *Beige Book* and find the latest economic information for your region of the country (see if you can find the *Beige Book* using one of the search engines).

Are economic conditions improving or worsening in your area?

What has happened to employment, incomes, and prices in your area recently?

What is the forecast for economic conditions in your area?

Next, compare the economic conditions in your region to those in the nation as a whole. Use the Internet to find economic forecasts for the national economy. How do you think your region will be affected by the forecasted conditions?

3.2 The Internet as an Economics Learning Tool: An Example

Now that you know where a variety of economics resources are located on the Internet, let's see how those resources can help you improve your economics skills. The best way to learn economics is to practice it, so we've created an assignment that illustrates how an economist might combine the information-gathering tools of the Internet with economic theory to solve a typical business problem.

Your Assignment: An Economic Forecast of Industry Sales

Let's say that at the start of the day your boss has called you into her office for an important meeting. She's going to be making a presentation to the company's top executives and needs (1) a summary of the current state of the national and regional economies, (2) a six-month forecast of future economic conditions, and (3) an analysis of how those conditions will affect industry sales—all by tomorrow! The executives are making a strategic business decision: whether to begin production of a major new line of furniture or postpone production until a later date. Making the right decision could increase sales and profits dramatically or, alternately, save the company millions of dollars in unsold inventory.

You've got a day to put together this summary, but where to begin? The solution to this problem involves a number of steps: (1) gathering information about current economic activity, (2) combining that information with economic theory to construct a forecast of future economic conditions, and (3) determining how expected future conditions will affect company sales.

The First Stage: Gathering Your Data

For this project you'll need to find as much information as you can about current and projected economic conditions in your area and in the nation—statistics like retail sales, employment, inflation rates, interest rates, income, and new housing starts. In addition, you'll need to determine what "story" these statistics are telling: Is the economy in a recession? Is economic activity slowing or accelerating? Is inflation a problem? How is the Federal Reserve likely to respond? Are interest rates likely to fall or rise during the coming months?

Start by looking at Internet sites that present recent economic statistics, as well as the Federal Reserve's *Beige Book,* to get a feel for current regional and national economic conditions. On-line magazines such as *Fortune* or *Business Week* often provide additional insights about recent trends in the economy, and some banks provide economic analyses and forecasts on the Internet. Next, use a search engine to find still more information, perhaps using keywords such as "economy," "current economic conditions," "Federal Reserve," and "economic forecasts." This is the data-gathering stage of your task, and this is where the Internet is most useful.

The Next Step: Forecasting Future Economic Activity

After obtaining a broad set of information on economic conditions, you need to analyze this information and concisely summarize your conclusions. Are the economic statistics you gathered telling a consistent story, or are various economic indicators giving you conflicting information? Do you need to gather additional data? Next, you need to determine how your information fits in with economic theory. If inflation rates are increasing, is it due to expanding consumer demand or a rise in input prices, such as the price of oil? If the economy is slowing, what is causing the slowdown, a drop in consumer or business purchases? Understanding the underlying causes of current economic conditions may help you predict important policy responses by the government or the Federal Reserve.

Next, using economic theory to organize your information, construct a forecast of expected future economic conditions, taking into account any policy actions the Federal Reserve or the government might take.

Putting it All Together: Predicting Future Company Performance

Finally, what are the implications of this information for your industry and company? For example, if the economy seems to be gaining momentum, but inflation is beginning to increase, how is the Federal Reserve likely to react? Is the Federal Reserve likely to raise interest rates or leave them alone? Interest rates play an important role in determining new home sales and the pace of new home buying is important for the furniture industry. If the Federal Reserve raises interest rates, for example, the resulting slowdown in home sales will likely translate into fewer orders for new furniture.

At this point you're ready to summarize your economic analysis and present it to your boss. If your projections are consistent with economic theory and are supported by the data you have collected, you can be confident that you have made the best forecast possible. It pays to go back over your analysis to make sure you have been thorough—a business decision based on incomplete analysis could have disastrous effects on your company and leave you without a job.

What Have You Learned?

What does an exercise like this teach you? First, the Internet can significantly reduce the amount of time it takes to gather information. Without the Internet, gathering the required information would be a formidable and time-consuming task. It would require looking in multiple sources—magazines, newspapers, trade publications, government documents—and would most likely involve a trip to the library. Second, the Internet is a learning *tool,* not a substitute for learning. At this time the Internet functions much like a library, putting an enormous amount of information at your fingertips. Economics is about learning to use that information to analyze, explain, and predict economic behavior. The Internet is a useful tool for gathering information, but making this information useful to your company also involves economic theory. Combining the two helps companies make better business decisions.

3.3 Using the Internet to Help You Learn Economics: More Ideas

The exercise in the last section gives you a feel for how you can put the Internet to work for you in your economics course. In this section we present some additional ideas to illustrate how you might use the Internet to deepen and broaden your understanding of economics. Again, we have chosen to be selective rather than encyclopedic, and in many cases the ideas reflect our own teaching backgrounds. We encourage you to construct your own strategies for using the Internet to enhance your understanding of economics. One of the virtues of the Internet is that it is a learning tool that can be used in many different ways.

As you might guess, many of the ideas listed here focus on using the Internet as an information-gathering tool. As you gather information from Internet sites around the world, try to relate this information to the economic concepts you are learning in the classroom. The more ways that you can connect these economic concepts to the real world, the more you will understand about economics and the longer you will retain this knowledge.

Linking Current Events and Economic Theory

Because information on the Internet can be updated almost continuously, the Internet provides an ever-changing sea of information about current economic and business events. Visit on-line business news sites, magazines, and newspapers frequently to obtain the latest news and information about the economy, businesses, and financial markets. The *Wall Street Journal* provides an Internet page listing economics-related articles (including page numbers) in that day's print version of the paper. An on-line version of the paper is also available for a fee.

Try to link the news stories you find to the economic theory you are learning in your economics course. Talk to other students about the stories you have read and see if they can provide new economic insights you may have overlooked. Discussing real-world events in the classroom or during informal conversations with friends helps bring economic theory alive and helps you make connections between economic theory and the real world.

Your Turn

Visit one of the Web sites listed in section 3.1 that provides current business news.

What economics/business stories are making headlines today?

How are these stories related to the economic theory that you are learning in your economics course?

Exploring Economic Policy Issues

Analyzing current economic policy issues also provides an opportunity to try out your economic skills. *The Economic Report of the President,* as well as articles from *Business Week, Fortune,* and *The Economist* often provide in-depth discussions of important economic policy issues. For an in-depth discussion of policy issues also try some of the economic policy institute Web sites listed in the first section of this chapter. Use your economic theory to analyze the arguments that are made in the policy papers you find there. How do political considerations affect the economic policy conclusions that the writers come up with?

Your Turn

Find an Internet site that contains information about one of the following policy issues (use a search engine or the sites listed in the first section of this chapter) and use economic analysis to determine the validity of any claims that are made. How can you use these issues as case studies to help you understand particular economic concepts such as economic growth and the role of the government in the economy?

Flat Tax Proposal

Privatizing Social Security

Balanced Budget

Welfare Reform Environmental Policy Antitrust Policy

What other topics can you think of? Look at chapter section headings, examples, and *key words* in your textbook for additional ideas. Do an Internet search to see what you can find out about these issues and how they are related to economics.

Analyzing Economic Data

To supplement the diagrams in your textbook, retrieve economic data and use a spreadsheet program such as Excel or Lotus to analyze and view them. Do the data support the economic theories presented in your textbook?

Your Turn

Look up data on the Consumer Price Index (CPI) and use this data to calculate U.S. inflation rates over the past 20 years. Compare inflation rates in the U.S. to inflation rates in other countries, using data obtained from the Internet. What are the economic links between the U.S. and foreign economies that led to this behavior? What other economic statistics could you compare across countries?

3.4 Selected Activities from Prentice Hall's "PHLIPping Through the News"

Web-related activities are a great way to learn economics, especially when they combine real-world economic events and economic theory. Prentice Hall's *PHLIPping Through the News* (*http://wwwph-lip.marist.edu/pheconomics/current.htm*) Web site features biweekly summaries of economic news stories, along with related group activities, research ideas, and discussion questions. PHLIP stands for Prentice Hall's Learning on the Internet Partnership and is a dynamic Web site supplying up-to-date information on economics and business-related issues to accompany Prentice Hall textbooks.

We have included a sample of suggested activities from past articles to spur your imagination. See what other types of activities you can come up with, and check the PHLIP site regularly for new articles and ideas! Suggest one of these projects to your teacher—who knows, he or she may give you extra credit for carrying it out!

Predicting Federal Reserve Policy

You can involve the entire class in this project. Simulate a Federal Open Market Committee (FOMC) meeting by breaking the class into groups, each representing a different Federal Reserve district (or group of districts). In addition, select one of the groups to represent the Board of Governors and its chairman, Alan Greenspan. Have each group research current economic conditions in its respective Federal Reserve district(s) (use the Federal Reserve's *Beige Book, (http://www.bog.frb.fed.us/fomc/bb/ current/)* that provides up-to-date economic information about each district) and provide a written summary of its findings. In addition, have the group representing the Board of Governors research current *national* economic conditions (see Scott Simkins' *ECONlinks* site *(http://aurora.ncat.edu/~simkinss/ econlinks.html)* for links to current economic data) and provide a separate written report. After the summaries are written, bring the groups together to simulate an FOMC meeting. Each group should report on the conditions in its district, with the Board of Governors group reporting on national economic trends. Based on current economic conditions, make a prediction about *future* economic trends and come to a consensus on the appropriate monetary policy to follow for the next six months. To make the project more interesting, run it at the same time that the FOMC is actually preparing for an upcoming policy meeting. Compare your policy recommendations to those reached by the FOMC.

Computing Stock Market Returns in U.S. and Foreign Markets

Are you better off investing money in the U.S. stock market or a foreign stock market? To provide some perspective on this question, compare the returns you could earn in the U.S. stock market (using the Dow Jones Industrial Average index) with those you could earn in a foreign stock market (use a foreign stock market index such as the Tokyo Nikkei 225 or the London FT 100). How do the foreign returns differ when measured in dollars rather than the local currency?

First, use the World Wide Web to get daily closing values of your selected stock indexes over a two-month period. You can obtain domestic and foreign stock market information from the following sites:

http://www.bloomberg.com/
http://www.cnnfn.com/markets/

In addition, obtain the daily exchange rate (against the dollar) for the country whose foreign stock market index you are monitoring, in terms of the U.S. dollar. Express the values of the foreign stock market index in U.S. dollar values by dividing the foreign stock market index by the current exchange rate, measured in units of foreign currency per dollar. At the end of the two-month period, chart the index values of (1) the U.S. stock market, (2) the foreign stock market (measured in local foreign currency), and (3) the foreign stock market (measured in U.S. dollar). In what ways are the graphs similar or different?

Compare the returns in the foreign stock market to those in the U.S. stock market. Why are the foreign stock market returns, measured in local currency terms, different from those measured in U.S. dollar terms? What role do fluctuations in the exchange rate play? Based on this exercise, if you were an investor trying to decide whether to invest in U.S. or foreign stock markets, what factors would you need to consider?

Balance the Federal Budget

Can you balance the budget? What programs would you cut? You can take a try at balancing the U.S. federal budget using the University of California at Berkeley's *National Budget Simulator* (*http://garnet.berkeley.edu:3333/budget/budget.html*). The simulator actually uses the 1995 federal budget figures, but it will give you a good feel for the tradeoffs involved in moving toward a balanced budget.

Before you get started with a budget-cutting frenzy, familiarize yourself with the federal budget and the budget-making process using *A Citizen's Guide to the Federal Budget.* This guide contains information on sources of government revenue, government spending by category, recent data on budget deficits, and the budget-making process. You can access this information at *http://www.access.gpo.gov/omb/omb003.html.*

When you reach the site, you are asked to select a "database" and given the choice to enter keywords to search the database. Select *A Citizen's Guide to the Federal Budget* as the database and enter the keywords "table of contents." This will bring up a page of links that include the table of contents. Click on this link and you will see the individual chapters of the *Guide* listed. Next, go back to the search form and enter the title of one of the chapters to get access to the content from that chapter. You can also download the full text of the *Citizen's Guide* in Adobe Acrobat format, but you will need the Adobe Acrobat Reader software to view the files. This software is free on the Internet (*http://www.adobe.com/prodindex/acrobat/readstep.html*) and, once installed, is automatically linked to your browser.

After reading through the *Guide,* access the *National Budget Simulator* Web site. What would it take to balance the budget, given the present size of the budget deficit? What areas would you cut? Would you raise taxes? Be able to make a persuasive argument for your case.

You might try this with a group of students and compare your results. Have each student describe why he or she made particular cuts and keep a record of differences and similarities. How did the budget-cutting decisions differ? How would each person's budget cuts affect the economy in the future? What insights does this exercise provide into the difficulties Congress faces when making budget cuts?

Comparing Economic Growth in the U.S. and Asia

During the 1980s southeast Asian countries such as South Korea, Thailand, Hong Kong, and Taiwan—the "Asian Tigers"—saw their economies grow by more than 10% annually, leading to dramatic increases in economic development and living standards. Will such growth continue into the future, and will Asian economies bypass those of the U.S. on a per-capita basis? To gain some perspective on these questions, use the World Wide Web to obtain historical economic statistics. For example, see the Penn World Tables (foreign data) and the Economic Report of the President (U.S. data) to determine the

- level of per capita output (real output/population), in U.S. dollars, for one of the "Asian Tigers."
- annual growth rate of per capita output over the last 25 years.
- level of per capita output for the U.S.
- annual growth rate of per capita output over the last 25 years.

Using current per-capita output levels for the selected Asian country and the U.S., along with the growth rates you calculated, graph the *future paths* of per-capita output for the Asian country and the U.S. together on one graph. How many years will it take for the per-capita level of output in the Asian country to catch up with the U.S. level? What factors could affect the result?

3.5 Sources of Information for Graduate School, Law School, and Careers

For many of you, your undergraduate education is the first step toward the goal of a law degree, an MBA degree, or a graduate degree in economics. For others, an undergraduate degree may be the end of your formal training before you embark on your career. The Internet provides a number of Web sites to help you with career choices and to find a job, to prepare you for graduate school and law school admission tests, and to assist you in selecting graduate schools and programs that match your interests. To get you started, we have listed a few of these resources below.

Admissions Tests and Background Information

If you're thinking about graduate school or law school, look here for valuable information. These sites provide information on exam dates and registration deadlines, practice exams, on-line registration for tests, links to information about schools, programs, financial aid, and much more!

Graduate Record Exam (GRE)
  http://www.gre.com
Graduate Management Admissions Test (GMAT)
  http://www.gmat.org
Law School Admissions Test (LSAT)
  http://www.lsat.org
Princeton Review
  http://www.review.com
U.S. News Colleges and Careers Center
  http://www.usnews.com/usnews/edu/home.htm

Career and Job-Related Information on the Internet

Looking for a job? The Web sites below provide links to job listings, resume placement services, and career placement centers on the Internet. Many provide the ability to search by job type or geographical area, and some provide advice on putting together resumes and interviewing skills.

The Riley Guide: Employment Opportunities and Job Resources on the Internet
  http://www.jobtrak.com/jobguide/
Purdue University Placement Center
  http://www.ups.purdue.edu/Student/jobsites.htm
America's Job Bank
  http://www.ajb.dni.us/index.html
Links to Career Information Sites
  http://www.uncg.edu/csc/hotlink.htm
JobTrak
  http://www.jobtrak.com/
JobWeb
  http://www.jobweb.org/
Online Career Center
  http://www.occ.com/
StudentCenter
  http://www.studentcenter.com/

The Monster Board
   http://www.monster.com/
JobHunt
   http://www.job-hunt.org/
Job Resources by U.S. Region
   http://www.wm.edu/csrv/career/stualum/jregion.html
The Net Guide
   http://washingtonpost.com/parachute
CareerPath
   http://www.careerpath.com/
Equal Opportunity Publications
   http://www.eop.com/
FedWorld Federal Jobs Search
   http://www.fedworld.gov/jobs/jobsearch.html

3.6 Creating Your Own Web Page

There is no place like home, or your very own homepage. The following description will help you create one for yourself. It is not as simple as cruising the Web, but it isn't very hard. You can create a file on your home computer, or even on a floppy disk, that will act as a homepage. Ultimately, you will need access to a Web server to make your homepage part of the Internet. If your campus has a Web server, then there may be a place for student homepages. If you are using an Internet service provider to access the Web, then you will probably be able to post a homepage through that business at no additional cost. For the moment, though, let's focus on how to construct a homepage. You don't need to be able to post a homepage on a server to understand how to create one and use it.

What good is a homepage? You will find many uses for it. For example, you can use a homepage to organize important and frequently accessed links and bookmarks to the Internet. It can also keep you connected to business resources all over the world. Imagine designing a homepage and turning it in as homework. You could hand in an assignment that contains text as well as links to online data, additional resources, and pictures, and even an e-mail link so that the instructor can ask you a question!

As a starting point we have placed a sample home page on the Internet for you to copy and use. All you need to do is save the file to disk and personalize it using any word processor. After you have completed these steps you'll need to upload the home page back to your Internet service provider's site. *Voila,* you've got your own personal home page on the Web! After you become comfortable with the way Web pages are constructed you can create additional Web pages on your own.

Download Our Sample Home Page

In Chapter 2 we covered saving files to disk. Now we will put that knowledge to work. With Netscape (or any other browser) open, go to *http://www.prenhall.com/econsurfing/student.htm.* Following the instructions in Chapter 2, save the file to disk. You may change the name of the file as you wish, but we will refer to it as *student.htm* throughout this appendix. It's best to leave the *.htm* file extension as it is because it signals to the Web browser that this file needs to be processed as a Web page rather than as a file of text.

The *student.htm* file should look like the following:

```
<HTML>
<! ------------------------------ Beginning of Heading Section ------------------------------ >
<HEAD>
    <TITLE>Your Home Page </TITLE>
</HEAD>
<! ------------------------------ Beginning of Body Section ------------------------------ >
<BODY>
<CENTER>
    <H1>Your Name</H1>
    <H2>Your Title, Major, or Philosophy</H2>
    <H3>
        <ADDRESS>
            Your address<BR>
            May<BR>
            Go<BR>
            Here<BR>
        </ADDRESS>
    </H3>
</CENTER>
<HR>
<! ---------------------- Second Part of Body Section, Separated by Horizontal Line ---------------------- >
<DL>
    <H2>This is Your Life</H2>
    <DD>Just say something about yourself. You can include information about your interests and
hobbies or about your studies. You can also use the header size tags to make the text different sizes, as
was done in the name, title and address sections above.
    <P>
    <DD>You can have as many paragraphs as you wish. Here's another. Enjoy.
    <P>
</DL>
<HR> <! ---------------------- Third Part of Body Section, Separated by Horizontal Line ---------------------- >
<DL>
    <H2>Some Directories and Search Engines: </H2>
    <DD>
        <A HREF="http://www.infoseek.com">
            Infoseek Search Engine</a>
    <DD>
        <A HREF="http://www.excite.com">
```

```
            Excite Search Engine</a>
    <DD>
        <A HREF="http://www.Webcrawler.com/">
            <i>Web</i>Crawler Search Engine</A>
</DL>
<HR>
<!! -------------------- Fourth Part of Body Section, Separated by Horizontal Line! -------------------- >
    <H2>A Few Economics Sites: </H2>
    <DD>
        <A HREF="http://econwpa.wustl.edu/EconFAQ/EconFAQ.HTML">
            Bill Goffe's Resources for Economists on the Internet</A>
    <DD>
        <A HREF="http://www.elon.edu/users/o/econ/links">
            Jim Barbour's Economics Resources at Elon College</A>
    <DD>
        <A HREF="http://aurora.ncat.edu/~simkinss/econlinks.HTML">
            Scott Simkins' EconLinks at North Carolina A&T State University</A>
</DL>
<HR><! -------------------- Fifth Part of Body Section, Separated by Horizontal Line -------------------- >
<H3>
    Your Name <A HREF="mailto:Name@server.edu">E=mail address</A>
</H3>
</BODY>
<! -------------------- End of Body Section -------------------- >
</HTML>
```

Understanding HyperText Markup Language

Before we go any further, let's look at the structure of this file. If you understand how it works, you will find working with it easier to manage. The language this file is written in is called HyperText Markup Language, or HTML. HTML *commands* are included in brackets < > and tell your browser *how* to display the information. Markup languages are older than computers. In the days when newspapers were typeset by hand, markup editors took the text of news stories and "marked it up." They made marks, in a code which typesetters could read, which indicated type size, indentation, typeface (italic, bold, underline, and so on) and placement on the page. The marked-up text was then sent to the typesetters for printing.

When computers came along, the first word processors were simply automated markup editors. In the case of Web pages, markup language is still used so that any computer or browser can read the information and determine how to display the material. This provides the Web with its most powerful attribute: complete mobility across platforms.

Enough about the history, what about the file itself? There are three fundamental parts to any HTML file.

- First there is the <HTML> command at the top of the file. This lets your computer know that what follows is written in HTML.

- Then there is a section called the Header, indicated by the command <HEAD>.

- The third part is the body of the file itself, indicated by the command <BODY>.

Look back at the sample home page file we have provided. At the very top you'll see the <HTML> command. In the parlance of HTML, these commands called "tags." Tags always have a angle bracket (<) followed by one or more letters and a reverse angle bracket (>). They can appear in lowercase or uppercase in HTML documents. The <HEAD> and <BODY> commands listed above are examples of HTML tags.

Most HTML tags come in pairs. For example, the tag <HEAD>, found below the <HTML> tag at the beginning of the file, is accompanied by a corresponding </HEAD> tag two line below it. The second member of each tag pair has a forward slash (/) preceding the word to let the browser know that this is the end of a particular command. In this case, it tells the computer that this is the end of the header section of the document. Tags, when used in sets or pairs, surround a section of text and define the beginning and end of an HTML section. It is important to understand that tags can be used incorrectly, just as it is possible to use English incorrectly. If you forget to follow an HTML tag later with its corresponding mate, your file will look different than you expected when you view it via the browser. If that occurs, just go back and edit the HTML file until you correct the mistake.

In general, all HTML pages follow the same basic structure. Authors may add all sorts of bells and whistles to their pages, but all properly formatted Web pages must contain the following elements (in this order):

<HTML>
  <HEAD>

This is where a description and purpose of the page is written. The material is not viewed on the browser. This section is used only to document the intent of the page.

  </HEAD>
  <BODY>

This is where the material that is to be viewed through the browser will be written.

  </BODY>
</HTML>

Take a look back at our sample page and you will see that it follows this basic structure, although we have added additional text and tags in the body section of the file. You will also notice that not all of the tags operate in pairs; some are used singly. For example, note the use of the paragraph tag, <P>, in the second section of the document. This tag is used to separate sections of text with two spaces, and has no matching tag accompanying it. You could also use two line break tags, <BR>, to accomplish the same thing. Also notice the use of the <HR> tag at the beginning of each new section within the <BODY> of the document. This tag is also used singly and produces a horizontal line across the viewed page.

What do the Other Tags Do?

Each of the three sections contains particular information. As mentioned above, the <HTML> and </HTML> tags must be the first and last lines of the file. They "bookend" the entire HTML file. Within the <HEAD> </HEAD> section you can place several things. The most important is the title of the document. This is the information that appears in the (usually) blue bar at the top of Netscape and is the information the bookmark uses for its name in your bookmark file. The largest section is the <BODY> </BODY> portion. This is where you put the main part of your page.

Most of the remaining tags are fairly self-explanatory. For example, <CENTER> centers the text, <H1>, <H2>, and so on set the text size for headings (1 is the largest, 6 the smallest), and <DL> begins a definition list (with <DD> indicating the definitions). Some of the tags stand alone. For example <HR> inserts a horizontal rule (a line) across the page, <P> indicates a paragraph break, and <DD> moves in one level in a delimited list.

The best way to learn what these tags do is to look at the "source" file, such as the one we have provided, and see how the information within different sections of the file appears in the Netscape browser. You can view the source file of any Web page by clicking on the *View* menu button and then selecting *Document Source* from the menu. You might want to print this file to make comparing the two easier. By editing the source file and seeing how the formatting changes on the browser screen you can quickly learn the basics of HTML authoring. The browser view of the beginning of the *student.htm* file is illustrated in Figure 13.

Creating Hyperlinks

One of the most important commands, and one that separates the Web from a paper-and-ink book, is the anchor tag, <A> </A>. This pair allows you to build hypertext, the "magical" links within a Web page. Let's dissect an anchor command:

```
<A HREF="http://www.infoseek.com">
    Infoseek Search Engine
</A>
```

The beginning tag <A> has a hypertext reference (HREF) in it. In this case it directs your browser to http://www.infoseek.com. Notice that the URL is enclosed in double quotes. Between the <A> and </A> commands comes the text that will show up on your Web page as a hyperlink, in this case "Infoseek Search Engine." Then comes the end of anchor tag </A>. That's all there is to it. It's really not magic at all.

Customizing Your Home Page

You can use any word processor or text editor to edit your home page source file. Simply open your text editor and load the file *student.htm* (or whatever you named your home page when you downloaded and saved it above). Treat it just as you would any other text document. If you use a *word processor,* such as Word or WordPerfect, make sure you save your file as a *text* document, not a Word or Word-Perfect document.

Make changes, rearrange, add, delete; generally fix it up so that it looks the way you want. As you are working on it, you can view how it will turn out by saving it back to disk and the loading it into Netscape using the *Open File* (Ctrl+O) command from the *File* menu button. If you set your text editor to run in one window and Netscape to run in another, you can easily flip back and forth to keep track of your progress.

When you are ready to add to your page using commands that are not included in this template, we recommend the following two references, both of which are included on the sample home page as links:

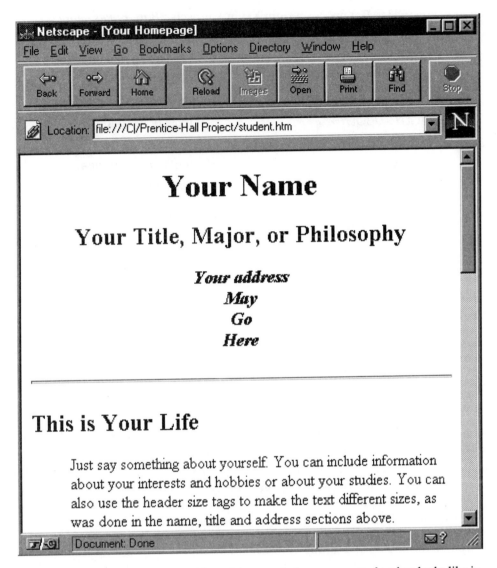

Figure 13. This is what the beginning of the sample home page *student.htm* looks like in Netscape. Compare this to the source file to determine how the HTML tags work.

The BareBones Guide to HTML
   http://werbach.com/barebones/
The Microsoft Web Authoring Guide
   http://www.microsoft.com/workshop/author/newhtml/default.htm
A Beginners Guide to HTML
   http://www.ncsa.uiuc.edu/General/Internet/WWW/HTMLPrimer.html

If you feel the need to have a reference book at your fingertips, there are several available in most book-stores. *Creating Your Own Netscape Web Pages* by Andy Shafran, and others from QUE Publishers (1995), provides an excellent beginner's reference.

Here is a small subset of common HTML tags taken from Kevin Werbach's *Bare Bones Guide:*

Document Type	<HTML></HTML>	(beginning and end of file)
Title	<TITLE></TITLE>	(must be in header)
Header	<HEAD></HEAD>	(descriptive information)
Body	<BODY></BODY>	(bulk of the page)
Heading	<H?></H?>	(sizes range from 1–6)
Bold	<B></B>	(bold,or heavy, type)
Italic	<I></I>	(italic type)
Font Size	<FONT SIZE=?></FONT>	(sizes range from 1–7)
Link Something	<A>HREF="*URL goes here*"></A>	
Display Image	<IMG SRC="*URL goes here*">	
Paragraph	<P>	(inserts blank line)
Horizontal Rule	<HR>	
Break	 	
Definition List	<DL>	(<DL>=definition list,
	<DT>	<DT>=term,
	<DD>	<DD>=definition)
	</DL>	

Once you have your home page the way you like it, simply save it to a floppy disk or your computer's hard drive as an ASCII or DOS text file and you will be ready to go. Remember to use the .htm or .html extension after your file name. The advantage of having your homepage on floppy disk is that you'll have a portable homepage that you can use on any computer. This is especially handy if you do most of your Web browsing in a university computer lab. If you work mainly on your own computer at home or in the dorm, then you'll want to save your homepage on your computer's hard drive.

Here is a five-step procedure for finding and setting your default homepage to the one you've created.

1. Copy your intended homepage to either a floppy disk or your hard drive.

2. With *Netscape,* find the command under the *File* menu called *Open File....* When you start this command, you'll get a dialog window where you can designate the file you wish to open. You want to open your homepage, which at the moment is not on a server. Select the HTML file for your homepage from either your floppy disk or hard drive, and press the Return key. Because your file is written in HTML, your browser will open up and display it for you.

3. If it isn't set already, change your Options setting so that you can view the URLs of the pages that display on your browser. When this is set properly, you'll notice that your file's URL is listed something like this: file:///............./file.html. The protocol is no longer HTTP, and there are more than two slashes.

4. Record this URL on a piece of paper so that you can refer to it in the next step. Every little slash and colon counts, so copy carefully to avoid a problem.

5. To change the homepage designation for your browser, open the *General Preferences* section of the *Options* menu. Select the *General* tab and enter the URL that you wrote down from step 4 into the homepage entry window.

Now that you've performed these steps, your browser should automatically jump you onto your homepage when you select the *Home* button from the toolbar. Give it a try. The procedures that you've just performed have allowed your browser to memorize the location of your homepage file. But remember, if you're working in a university computer lab, you'll probably have to repeat steps 4 and 5 each time you browse the Web.

A tip: If you put your bookmark file and your home page file on one disk, then any time you go to a lab to browse the Internet you will be able to load them from the disk and have your own customized workstation.

How Can I Let Everyone See My Creation?

To make your home page available for public viewing you will first need to upload your home page to an Internet Web server. On most campuses the computing center will provide space for student home pages on the campus Web server; it is probably connected to your e-mail account. Contact your university computer center for more information. Then upload the file from your floppy to the server and grant public rights to it. How you go about doing that will vary from place to place, but rest assured that if you walk into a computer lab on any campus in the country and strike up a conversation with the lab assistant or the person at the help desk, he or she can show you how it is done.

A couple of hints will make your home page more user-friendly: (1) put it in a sub-directory named *public_html* and (2) name it *index.html*—it will be easiest to access in this way. For example, assume you have an account in your name on an e-mail server and the address is *myname@thischool.edu*. If you create a public_html subdirectory under the account *myname,* place your home page in that subdirectory, and name it *index.html,* your Web address will be *http://www.thischool.edu/~myname/*. Of course this specific example doesn't apply to all systems, but the idea is the same: If you point a browser to a particular subdirectory and do not specify a file name, it will attempt to open a file named *index.html.*

Many universities also allow you to link your home page to the university's main Web page. This makes it easy for your friends to find your home page by simply connecting to the university home page and searching through the links provided there. To see whether this is possible at your university, check with the campus computing center.

Making Your Own Personal Economics Web Page

Now that you have the idea and have created your personal home page, experiment with putting links to other Web sites on your home page. You might start by using some of the economics links that are listed in the first section of this chapter. Before too long you will have not just a home page but a personal economics Web site.

Glossary

ActiveX

This is a resource developed by *Microsoft* to extend the function of their *Internet Explorer* software.

Archie

This is a search tool used to find resources that are stored on Internet-based FTP servers. Archie is short for Archive because it performs an archive search for resources (See *FTP* and *Server*.).

AVI

This stands for Audio/Video Interleaved. It is a Microsoft Corporation format for encoding video and audio for digital transmission.

Background

This refers to an image or color that is present in the background of a viewed Web document. Complex images are becoming very popular as backgrounds but require a great deal more time to download. The color of default background can be set for most Web browsers.

Bookmark

This refers to a list of URLs saved within a browser. The user can edit and modify the bookmark list to add and delete URLs as the user's interests change. Bookmark is a term used by Netscape to refer to the user's list of URLs; *Hotlist* is used by Mosaic for the same purpose (See *Hotlist, Mosaic,* and *URL*.).

Browser

This is a software program that is used to view and browse information on the Internet. Browsers are also referred to as clients (See *Client*.).

Bulletin Board Service

This is an electronic bulletin board. It is sometimes referred to as a BBS. Information on a BBS is posted to a computer where people can access, read, and comment on it. A BBS may or may not be connected to the Internet. Some are accessible by modem dial-in only.

Cache

This refers to a section of memory set aside to store information commonly used by the computer or by an active piece of software. Most browsers will create a cache for commonly accessed images. An example might be the images that are common to the user's homepage. Retrieving images from the cache is much quicker than downloading the images from the original source each time they are required.

Chat room

This is a site that allows for real-time person-to-person interactions.

Clickable image

(Clickable map) This refers to an interface used in Web documents that allow the user to click, or select, different areas of an image and receive different responses. Clickable images are becoming a popular way to offer a user many different selections within a common visual format.

Client

This is a software program used to view information from remote computers. Clients function in a Client-Server information exchange model. This term may also be loosely applied to the computer that is used to request information from the server (See *Server.*).

Compressed file

This refers to a file or document that has been compacted to save memory space so that it can be easily and quickly transferred through the Internet.

Download

This is the process of transferring a file, document, or program from a remote computer to a local computer (See *Upload.*).

E-mail

This is the short name for electronic mail. E-mail is sent electronically from one person to another. Some companies have e-mail systems that are not part of the Internet. E-mail can be sent to one person or to many different people (I sometimes refer to this type of mail as JunkE-mail.)

FAQ

This stands for Frequently Asked Questions. A FAQ is a file or document where a moderator or administrator will post commonly asked questions and their answers. Although it is very easy to communicate across the Internet, if you have a question, you should check for the answer in a FAQ first.

Forms

This refers to an interface element used within Web documents to allow the user to send information back to a Web server. With a forms interface, the user is requested to type responses within entry windows to be returned to the server for processing. Forms rely on a server computer to process the submittals. They are becoming more common as browser and server software improve.

FTP

This stands for *File Transfer Protocol*. It is a procedure used to transfer large files and programs from one computer to another. Access to the computer to transfer files may or may not require a password. Some FTP servers are set up to allow public access by anonymous log-on. This process is referred to as *Anonymous FTP.*

GIF

This stands for Graphics Interchange Format. It is a format created by CompuServe to allow electronic transfer of digital images. GIF files are a commonly-used format and can be viewed by both Mac and Windows users.

Gopher

Is a format structure and resource for providing information on the Internet. It was created at the University of Minnesota

GUI

Is an acronym for Graphical User Interface. It is a combination of the appearance and the method of interacting with a computer. A GUI requires the use of a mouse to select commands on an icon-based monitor screen. Macintosh and Windows operating systems are examples of typical GUIs.

Helper

This is software that is used to help a browser view information formats that it couldn't normally view.

Homepage

In its specific sense, this refers to a Web document that a browser loads as its central navigational point to browse the Internet. It may also be used to refer to as Web page describing an individual. In the most general sense, it is used to refer to any Web document.

Hotlist

This is a list of URLs saved within the Mosaic Web browser. This same list is referred to as a *Bookmark* within the Netscape Web browser.

HTML

An abbreviation for HyperText Markup Language, the common language used to write documents that appear on the World Wide Web.

HTTP

An abbreviation for HyperText Transport Protocol, the common protocol used to communicate between World Wide Web servers.

Hypertext

This refers to text elements within a document that have an embedded connection to another item. Web documents use hypertext links to access documents, images, sounds, and video files from the Internet. The term hyperlink is a general term that applies to elements on Web pages other than text.

Inline image

This refers to images that are viewed along with text on Web documents. All inline images are in the GIF format. JPEG format is the other common image format for Web documents; an external viewer is typically required to view such documents.

Java

This is an object-oriented programming language developed by *Sun Microsystems.*

JavaScript

This is a scripting language developed by *Netscape* in cooperation with *Sun Microsystems* to add functionality to the basic Web page. It is not as powerful as Java and works primarily from the client side.

JPEG

This stands for Joint Photographic Experts Group. It is also commonly used to refer to a format used to transfer digital images.

Jughead

This is a service for performing searches on the Internet (See *Archie* and *Veronica.*).

Mosaic

This is the name of the browser that was created at the National Center for Supercomputing Applications. It was the first Web browser to have a consistent interface for the Macintosh, Windows, and UNIX environments. The success of this browser is responsible for the expansion of the Web.

MPEG

This stands for Motion Picture Experts Group. It is also a format used to make, view, and transfer both digital audio and digital video files.

Newsgroup

This the name for the discussion groups that can be on the *Usenet*. Not all newsgroups are accessible through the Internet. Some are accessible only through a modem connection (See *Usenet.*).

Plug-in

This is a resource that is added to the Netscape to extend its basic function.

QuickTime

This is a format used by Apple Computer to make, view, edit, and send digital audio and video.

Server

This is a software program used to provide, or serve, information to remote computers. Servers function in a Client-Server information exchange model. This term may also be loosely applied to the computer that is used to serve the information (See *Client.*).

Table

This refers to a specific formatting element found in HTML pages. Tables are used on HTML documents to visually organize information.

Telnet

This is the process of remotely connecting and using a computer at a distant location.

Upload

This is the process of moving or transferring a document, file, or program from one computer to another computer.

URL

This is an abbreviation for Universal Resource Locator. In its basic sense it is an address used by people on the Internet to locate documents. URLs have a common format that describes the protocol for information transfer, the host computer address, the path to the desired file, and the name of the file requested.

Usenet

This is a world-wide system of discussion groups, also called newsgroups. There are many thousands of newsgroups, but only a percentage of these are accessible from the Internet.

Veronica

Believe it or not, this is an acronym. It stands for *Very Easy Rodent Oriented Net-wide Index to Computerized Archives*. This is a database of menu names from a large number of Gopher servers. It is a quick and easy way to search Gopher resources for information by keyword. It was developed at the University of Nevada.

VRML

This stands for Virtual Reality Markup Language. It was developed to allow the creation of virtual reality worlds. Your browser may need a specific plug-in to view VRML pages.

WAIS

This stands for Wide Area Information Servers. This is a software package that allows the searching of large indexes of information from the Internet.

WAV

This stands for Waveform sound format. It is a Microsoft Corporation format for encoding sound files.

Web (WWW)

This stands for the World Wide Web. When loosely applied, this term refers to the Internet and all of its associated incarnations, including Gopher, FTP, HTTP, and others. More specifically, this term refers to a subset of the servers on the Internet that use HTTP to transfer hyperlinked document in a page-like format.

Web Browser

This is the computer software needed to access the information available on the Internet. The most commonly used browsers are *Netscape Navigator* and *Microsoft Internet Explorer.*

Webmaster

The person responsible for maintaining (and often designing) the Web site of an organization.

Appendix 1

What You Need to Get Started at Home

Many of you will access the Internet from a campus computer network, in which case the necessary hardware and software should already be available. For those of you who will be accessing the Internet from home, we've summarized the basic equipment, service, and software that you'll need to get started browsing the Internet from your own computer. To get started, you'll need a *computer,* a *modem,* an *Internet connection,* and *browser software.* The descriptions that follow will help you understand each component and its function as you set up your own Internet access.

The Computer

Web-browsing software such as Netscape Navigator is available for both Macintosh and Windows-based operating systems, so whichever type of computer system you own, you should be able to access the Internet as long as your computer has the necessary power and memory. Basic system configurations for running the Netscape Navigator on Macintosh or Windows-based computers are listed below. Most new computers sold today have the necessary resources to run the latest versions of the browser software.

Macintosh

- 68030
- System 7.0
- 256 color monitor
- 16 MB of RAM
- a 28.8 kps (or higher) modem
- 8 MB of free disk space for browser software

PC-*Compatible*

- Intel 486
- Windows 3.1
- VGA monitor
- 16 MB of RAM
- a 28.8 kps (or higher) modem
- 8 MB of free disk space for browser software

Recently the Network Computer, or NC, has begun springing up. An NC is a computer without what you would expect in a computer: word processing, drawing, graphing, and number crunching. (Because these features may be helpful in your education, you should consider carefully whether to buy only an NC instead of a full computer.) The NC and similar products allow you to connect your television directly to the Internet. *WebTV* is currently the most popular product, but there will probably be others brands to choose from in the near future. The advantage to such products is that they are much cheaper than a full-blown computer and you don't have to be a computer genius to use them.

Modems

Unless you have a direct connection to the Internet through a business or university, you'll need a modem to connect your computer to an Internet service provider over telephone lines. When it comes to buying modems, buy something as fast as possible but not a modem of less than 28,400 (28.8 K) baud rate. The baud rate is a measure of the speed at which the modem transfers data. The higher the number, usually the faster the transfer rate. With a typical 28.8K baud modem you can expect that it will take a few seconds to transfer a typical Web page, but this will vary depending on the complexity of the page. Many computers sold today include a modem as part of the system package. Also, keep in mind that manufacturers will continue to introduce newer and faster modems as pages become more complex and slower to load, as technology increases, and as users demand faster speeds.

The Internet Connection

Some campuses, although lacking a walk-in lab, have made arrangements for students to dial into the campus computer system, and through it to the Internet, from home or a dorm room with a modem. If this is the case, then search out the campus computing center to find out the specifics of how you can access this service.

Most people who access the Internet from their homes subscribe to an Internet service provider such as America Online, Compuserve, Microsoft Network, or one of the many other local and national companies selling access to the Internet. You must pay a monthly fee to the company, which allows you to access the Internet for a specified number of hours via a telephone connection. Some of these providers, such as America Online, allow you to access proprietary material as well as the resources available on the Internet.

The market for Internet service provision is very competitive, and you should shop around for the best deals. Search the Internet to contact national service providers; local Internet service providers are listed in your phone book. Most Internet service providers give you limited free connection time to evaluate their service. Take advantage of these offers and consider not only the monthly fees, but also the accessibility, the ability to use independent browser software (such as Netscape Navigator), and the ease of use. Here are a few things to consider when choosing an Internet service provider (ISP).

Does the ISP have a local number for your area? You need to call the provider each time you access the Internet. Paying a toll call every time you do so will cost you a ton of money if you use the Internet regularly.

Can their system handle a large number of simultaneous connections? Ask them how many users they can handle at one time and how many subscribers they have. Although they may have a reasonable price and a local number, it doesn't mean much if you can't get on to use it. If after you subscribe you find that you are never able to connect or that the only available access is late at night or early in the morning, then find a new ISP.

Do they offer SLIP/PPP connections? This is the type of connection that you'll need if you want to use a graphical browser like *Netscape Navigator* or *Internet Explorer.* Some ISP's only offer shell accounts. Shell accounts require you to type in each command as you would with DOS. It is somewhat like driving a horse and buggy when everyone else has an automobile.

Do they have a reasonable monthly subscription fee? Cheapest is not always best. The added features and the staffing support are important points to consider when choosing a service. Some Internet service providers offer you unlimited monthly connect time at a flat fee, and others offer you a per-hour fee with additional hours costing extra. You will need to estimate your expected usage and purchase accordingly. Ask if there is a fee to upgrade your service if you find that you need more time. If you have a roommate, then consider upgrading the service and splitting the cost. This may actually save you money.

Does your ISP include the Internet browser software in the price? You'll find that not all do. Most ISP's have an agreement with either *Netscape* or *Microsoft* to bundle their browser software. The provided software may also be partially configured to work on the ISP's system, so you'll be much farther along by using it and the technicians will be better able to help you with a problem.

Is the ISP a regional or local company? This may not be important to everyone, but for you who go home during holidays or travel far and wide during vacations, you may be quite far from campus. If the ISP covers a wide enough area, then you can still check your e-mail and cruise the Net when you are away from school.

Do they have a help line in case you need technical assistance to set up your connection? Call the help line before you subscribe and make sure you talk to a real person. Although you may be asked to leave your name and number, you should expect to get a return call within 24 hours. If they don't return your call within this time period, then the service is probably understaffed or poorly managed.

Does the ISP offer both newsgroup and e-mail access in addition to a connection to the Web? This is usually standard but there are always exceptions; it is better to ask up front.

Does it cost you extra for additional e-mail addresses? If you have a roommate, then you may find that it is more affordable to split the cost of a subscription and pay for an additional e-mail account.

Will your ISP add newsgroups at your request? Most ISP's subscribe to a small fraction of the available newsgroups, and you may find that they don't include some of the basic, business-oriented groups that your instructors may recommend. It shouldn't cost anything for the ISP to add these groups to their list.

Does the ISP offer you space for your own Web page? Often, one of the features offered in the basic package is the option of constructing and posting your own page. The ISP usually sets a memory usage limit that affects the total size of the page and its traffic flow (that is, the number of people viewing the site).

The most important thing to remember when using an Internet service provider is to expect courteous and prompt service. If you don't like what you are paying for, then cancel and go somewhere else. There are plenty of competitors willing to offer you better service.

The Web Browser Software

If everything has fallen into place, you should now have access to a computer with enough power to run the browser software and a connection to the Internet, either through your school or an Internet service provider. There's only one thing left for you to obtain—the Web browser software. In this book we chose to focus on Netscape Communication's *Netscape Navigator* software for the simple reason that it currently commands the greatest market share among available Web browsers and is the browser you are most likely to see installed on university computers. Microsoft's *Internet Explorer* is another popular Web browser that comes pre-installed on all new personal computers running the Windows95 operating system. Both are good all-around Web browsers that are updated regularly. Best of all, these Web browsers (and others) are available ***free of charge*** over the Internet! All you need to do is download the appropriate files and install them on your machine. Instructions are included at the Internet site to make this process as simple as possible. Once you have all of these basic elements and they've been put together correctly, you'll be ready to start traveling on the Internet.

We have included the Web addresses below to help make your access to the Internet and the World Wide Web as smooth as possible. Check out the information at these sites to help you select Web browser software, an Internet service provider, and a new computer. A little bit of research and planning beforehand can save a lot of time and frustration later.

The Browser Software

Right now you should have a computer and a modem. Use the following Internet addresses to research the right browser for you.

Netscape Navigator
http://www.netscape.com
Microsoft Internet Explorer
http://www.microsoft.com

The Internet Service Provider

Now, with your computer, modem, and browser, you're only one step away. Use the following Internet addresses to research the right ISP for you. You might want to consider the questions I outlined previously.

Choosing the Internet
http://home.netscape.com/
Service Provider *Netscape*
assist/isp_select/index.html
Internet Access
http://www.liii.com/~dhjordan/students
Provider Guide
/docs/welcome.htm
Choosing An Internet Provider
http://tcp.ca/Dec95/Commtalk_ToC.html

Doing Your Homework

It is always nice to have an independent opinion. In addition to talking with friends who are experienced with computers and the Internet, read what the critics have to say. Stop by the following Internet addresses and visit the largest publishers of computer-related magazines. Between them, they print nearly 50 different popular periodicals about computers and the Internet. Search their databases for articles that will help you decide what computer and software to buy. You can read the articles online.

CMP Media Inc.'s(Publisher of Windows Magazine and others)
http://www.techweb.com/info/publications/publications.html
Ziff Davis (Publisher of PC Magazine, MacUser, and others)
http://www5.zdnet.com/findit/search.html

Appendix II

Sending and Retrieving Internet Mail

Effective learning involves communication among instructors and students. Netscape and many other browsers have incorporated the ability to communicate with other students and your instructors using electronic mail, or e-mail. It's a wonderful way to exchange information, ask questions, and converse with others, especially when time or distance don't allow you to meet with someone face-to-face. In addition, e-mail links are built into many Web pages and allow you to send correspondence directly to others on the Internet.

E-mail Accounts

E-mail works through a mail *server* operated and maintained by the administrator of your campus computer network or by your Internet service provider. In general, the mail server is like your postal mailbox. The mailbox (server) is where mail addressed to you is stored until you pick it up. Before you can send or receive e-mail you will need to have an account (or address) on an e-mail server. Access to an e-mail server is available through your campus computing center or through your Internet service provider. If you are at a campus that has provided you with Internet access, ask the computing center how to apply for an e-mail account. If you obtain Internet access from a private service, you probably already have an e-mail account, whether you know it or not.

E-mail Addresses

When you receive your e-mail account you will be given a *username* that will uniquely identify you on the mail server. Your full e-mail address will include both your username and the name of the mail server. Here is the format of a typical e-mail address: USERNAME@HOST. DOMAIN. It is not necessary to have a full name for the NAME part of the address and, in fact, some addresses use only numbers to represent an individual. The @ symbol always follows the individual's name, and then comes the name of the mail server computer (HOST). The domain in the e-mail format, just like the domain of the URL format, is used to denote the affiliation of the user. Notice that there are no spaces anywhere in an e-mail address.

Using Netscape to Send and Retrieve Internet Mail

Current versions of Netscape allow you to use the browsing software to send and retrieve Internet mail. However, there are a couple of things that you'll need to do to properly configure your browser for sending e-mail. First, click on the *Options* menu button in Netscape and then select *Mail and News Preferences*. Click on the *Servers* tab and enter the name of the mail server (generally the "outgoing" and "incoming" mail servers are the same) and your assigned username for this server. You can also set the mail directory where Netscape will store your mail, as well as how often Netscape checks for new mail. Figure 14 illustrates the appearance of the dialog box that you have selected.

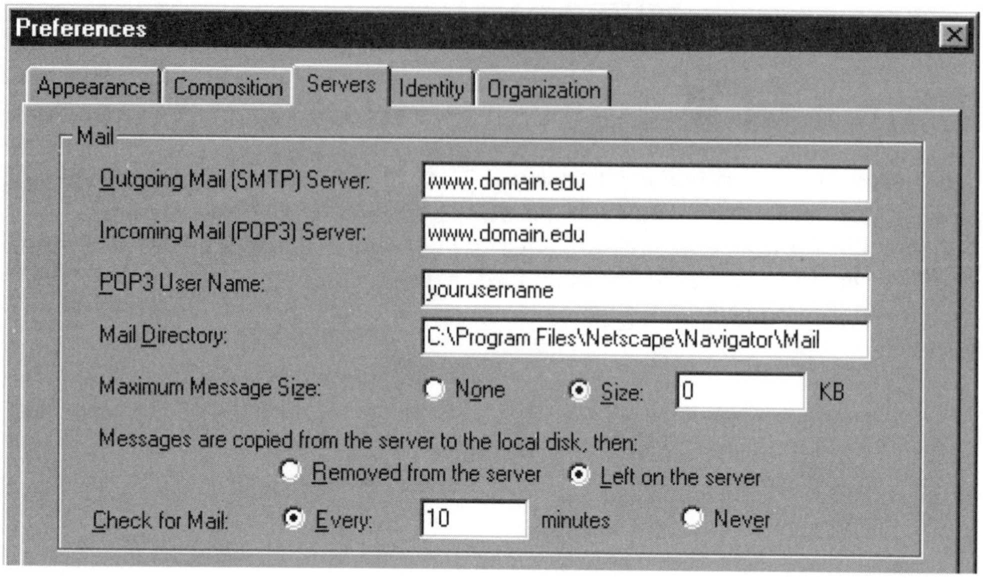

Figure 14. You must enter information about your mail server and *username* before you can use Netscape to send and retrieve e-mail.

Next, click on the *Identity* tab and enter your name and *full* e-mail address (see Figure 15 for an illustration) before clicking the *OK* button. After restarting the browser program you should be able to send and retrieve e-mail using Netscape.

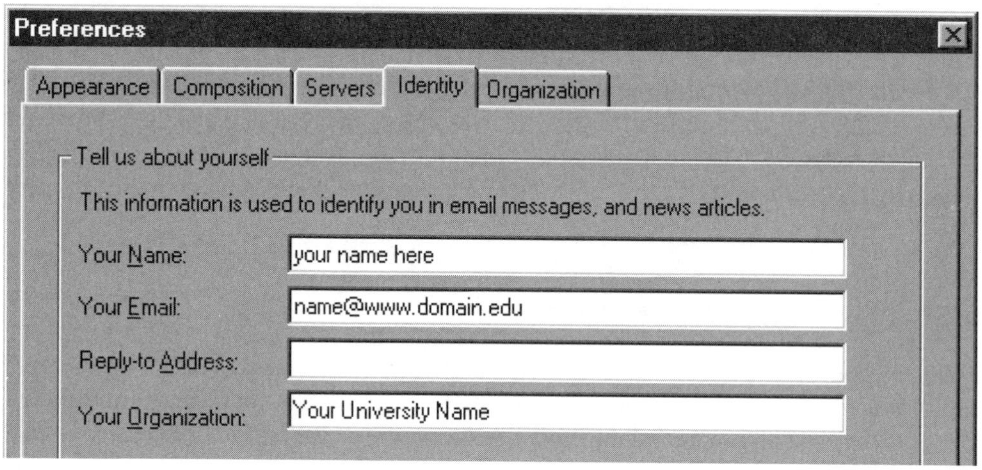

Figure 15. Filling in this information will identify you to the person receiving your mail.